RUDOLF STEINER (1861–1925) called his spiritual philosophy 'anthroposophy', meaning 'wisdom of the human being'. As a highly developed seer, he based his work on direct knowledge and perception of spiritual dimensions. He initiated a modern and universal 'science of spirit', accessible to anyone willing to exercise clear and unprejudiced thinking.

From his spiritual investigations Steiner provided suggestions for the renewal of many activities, including education (both general and special), agriculture, medicine, economics, architecture, science, philosophy, religion and the arts. Today there are thousands of schools, clinics, farms and other organizations involved in practical work based on his principles. His many published works feature his research into the spiritual nature of the human being, the evolution of the world and humanity, and methods of personal development. Steiner wrote some 30 books and delivered over 6000 lectures across Europe. In 1924 he founded the General Anthroposophical Society, which today has branches throughout the world.

THE IMAGINATIVE LIFE TABLEAU

The spiritually-perceived story of our life between birth and death

Meditative Knowledge Out of Childhood Forces

RUDOLF STEINER

Selected texts with commentary by Andreas Neider

Translated by Elizabeth Marshall

RUDOLF STEINER PRESS

Rudolf Steiner Press,
Hillside House, The Square
Forest Row, RH18 5ES

www.rudolfsteinerpress.com

Published by Rudolf Steiner Press 2020

Originally published in German under the title *Das imaginative Lebenstableau: Meditative Erkenntnis aus Kindheitskräften* by Rudolf Steiner Verlag, Basel, in 2017

A catalogue record for this book is available from the British Library

Print book ISBN: 978 1 85584 572 5
Ebook ISBN: 978 1 85584 509 1

Cover by Morgan Creative
Typeset by DP Photosetting, Neath, West Glamorgan
Printed and bound by 4Edge Ltd., Essex

Contents

Introduction

This compilation of texts bears the title 'The Imaginative Life Tableau' and deals with a subject which until now has received little attention. This is perhaps because in Rudolf Steiner's work the imaginative life tableau as a 'first result' of anthroposophical meditation—and this is what we are concerned with here—is only mentioned relatively late, not until the lectures of the year 1920 and then repeatedly until 1924. But what does he mean by this life tableau?

Those who have already studied anthroposophy will initially recognize what Steiner has often described as the first experience of human beings after death. For when the etheric body, the astral body and the I have left the physical body after death, then the person who has died sees their own etheric body before them. Everything the person has carried in themselves all their lives as the content of their consciousness and has stored in the form of memory is contained therein. But not only that, their etheric body was also the[1] sustainer of life, indeed the generator of that life and thus encompasses all the life forces out of which the dead person had shaped their life.

This life tableau belongs to the after-death experiences and in the first three days after death it gives the person who has died a panoramic overview of the life they have lived. It can however emerge as a result of the first level of meditation, imagination. Steiner spoke about this explicitly only from 1920 onwards.[2] In all the early depictions of meditation, for example in *An Outline of Esoteric Science*, he describes this experience as a conscious self-perception of the soul, which takes place in the world of images. In this inner encounter we are confronted in the spiritual world by our doppelgänger and, as a consequence of this harrowing experience, transforming this double becomes our most urgent task.[3]

In the relevant descriptions of the anthroposophic path of meditation from 1920 on, it is the understanding and realizing of our own life path which make possible the soul's encounter with itself in imagination. 'When you have attained imaginative cognition', he says, 'then you are able to see your own life story, what you have experienced from childhood until the present moment, as if in one piece, as if in a time tableau. You see constant movement, developing and becoming, as your own life story.' What you have here is 'as real as the growth forces, the life forces, which cause the whole soul configuration to unfold out of the body of the small child'. These are the processes and developments of the etheric organism.[4]

How could it be that Rudolf Steiner describes this first experience of the imaginative level of meditation in so many different ways without himself commenting on this double nature? This seems at first to be a discrepancy.

In order to answer this question, we have to look at the character of the etheric body or rather the etheric forces which permeate it. The human etheric body has namely two sides: on the one side it sustains the physical body as a living organism. At work here are the formative and growth forces which are strongest at the beginning of earthly life and are already functioning in the embryonic phase. According to Steiner some of these forces emancipate themselves as we grow older and become 'forces of thinking' and these are 'those forces which generate the shadowy world of thought for ordinary consciousness'.[5]

Thus, we can call one part of the etheric body the 'life aspect' and the other the 'consciousness aspect', or to go even further, one side as the female-nourishing aspect, the other as the male-enlightening aspect. And the astral body also has in this sense two sides: the one consciously active in thinking, the other unconsciously in willing.

This is also the reason why the anthroposophic path of meditation consists of two sorts of exercises. Steiner describes the one sort explicitly as 'meditation' and gives numerous exercises: either a mantram, which you have to engage with in thought, or an observation of nature or an image which you have to envisage. The other kind of exercises are aimed at the will. Here you usually begin with the retrospect exercise. Then the 'supplementary exercises', for example the eightfold way or the so called sixfold path.[6]

Clearly, Rudolf Steiner described the two sides of the etheric body and our experience of them through meditation and supplementary exercises at different times in his life's work, at first, more the male or consciousness side, then from 1920 onwards the female side, to which he related equally well but in a more intimate, occult manner.

Both of these forms lead us to deeper self-knowledge, which reveals on the one hand the shadow aspects of our own character in relation to our thinking, on the other, on the side of the life tableau—more the will aspect, the way in which our own lives have developed and unfolded. The imaginative experience of the consciousness aspect, which Steiner talked about extensively in his early depictions, leads to the experience of the doppelgänger, whereas the imaginative experience of the life aspect of the etheric body leads to the experience of the life tableau, as he described it from 1920 on, in various lectures you will find collected in this volume.

In his descriptions it is striking that he often links this experience of the life tableau with the still unconscious experiences of the small child. Steiner's remarks in this regard offer a point of contact with current discourse in psychotherapy. There has been a great deal of discussion recently about the 'inner child' and in modern psychotherapeutic practice, which is often inspired by Eastern ideas[7], the aim is to reach a reconciliation with this inner child. The corresponding psychotherapeutic approach caught on after the publication in 1990 of the book by Erika Chopich and Margaret Paul, *Healing Your Aloneness: Finding Love and Wholeness through Your Inner Child* and since then has become one of the most sought-after therapy models there are.[8]

What is the 'reconciliation with the inner child'? On the one hand it's about reclaiming the wonder and enthusiasm of the small child. On the other hand, about people bringing into focus the wounds, the injuries and the traumas, which they went through as small children, the suffering from too little attention, unfulfilled needs or too little love, and then through empathy and insight liberating themselves from the negative self-images, which developed out of such experiences. However, this form of therapy relies heavily on the usual memory images, which are intended to be laid bare and then experienced in a new way and thus liberated from the darkness of the soul.

Studying Rudolf Steiner allows us to extend and complement this, as he took a different approach. Steiner views conventional consciousness as fundamentally restricted and aims to take both thinking and the faculty of memory to a higher level through meditation. The basis for this is, as mentioned earlier, knowledge of the double nature of the etheric, through which, on the one hand, our physical bodies are shaped and formed and which, on the other hand, expresses itself in our soul lives as thinking.

Because the faculty of memory isn't connected as you would expect with the consciousness side, but with the will or life side of the etheric body,[9] through anthroposophic meditation Steiner shows us a way to gain access to both the etheric aspect of our thinking and, above all, to the living aspect of our memories. Thus in 1920 Steiner already emphasizes the following: 'Only by progressing to imagination can a psychology which goes beyond mere verbalism develop, a psychology which can really see into people.'[10]

It seems to me that until now even anthroposophic psychotherapy has hardly addressed or developed Steiner's imaginative approach, which we must clearly differentiate from the therapy methods mentioned above.[11] Possibly this is because Steiner long spoke of the life tableau only in connection with after-death experience and not until 1920 did he describe it as an imaginative perception which we should evoke during meditation. In the text extracts from the work of Rudolf Steiner presented here, the focus is on the life tableau developed in meditative work and thus on the turn-around of our line of vision from after death to before birth.

In the framework of his descriptions of the imaginative life tableau—and I want to accentuate this here—Steiner develops a distinctly Platonic orientated perspective on life before birth, which we can contrast with the often presented Aristotelian-Thomistic view of life after death. There we can find further links to contemporary psychotherapy approaches. For example, to the concept of the 'enneagram', which has been widespread since the 1970s and is connected to Neoplatonic thinking. In spiritually oriented psychotherapy work the enneagram is used today to create a kind of tableau of the soul in its earthly development. For example, it is deployed by A. H. Almaas, who describes in his essay 'Facets of Unity' how, through the enneagram, which represents in a certain way the earthly image of the soul, we can ascend to the 'holy ideas' which lie behind it.[12]

Now back to Steiner and his description of the imaginative life tableau. According to Steiner, as we have already seen, through imagination we can achieve a supersensible view of our own life story and its development. But that's not all. If we continue with our meditative work, we will, through inspiration, be able to look into the world which our soul descended from before birth and into the original oneness of the soul with this supersensible, soul-spiritual world. This is the world of 'holy ideas' in the Neoplatonic terminology of Almaas.

In the 'French course' which Steiner gave in September 1922 he links this insight gained through inspiration with 'philosophy'. Such a philosophy, which deals with the soul's descent, development of supersensible cognition and then re-ascent, is in direct succession to Plato, especially in the work of Plotinus (205–270), even if Steiner doesn't mention it here. Plotinus saw philosophy as an elixir in the sense that it is the re-ascent of the soul to its original unity.[13]

In the French course Steiner gives the idea of the descent of the soul described by Plotinus, which is at heart closely related to Eastern thinking, probably such a pivotal position because he could relate it to the philosophy of Bergson, who would have been well known to the French audience. He mentions Bergson several times during the course.[14] Bergson was familiar with Plotinus's philosophy, in particular with his idea of time as a continuum, which he then himself conceived of as 'durée', an idea which became very well known. Steiner discusses this idea of 'durée' in detail and contrasts it with his own concept of the imaginative review of one's own life-story as a tableau of the development of the soul in earthly existence.[15]

The imaginative experience of the life tableau and subsequently of inspirative cognition can be very productive as a meditative approach to the liberation of the soul from attachment in the context of psychotherapeutic work. I hope this has become clear through the points I made above. However, we must consider another aspect, which is important for soul work: the relationship between life and memory.

Rudolf Steiner describes the experience of 'bygone earthly life' in his written summary of the French course as follows: 'We see this like thought shapes which are densified into forces of growth. We don't just have the memory images of our own lives before us. We have images of an actual etheric process before us, which has played out in our own being without having risen into our ordinary consciousness. What lives in our consciousness and in memory is only the abstract by-product of the real process. In a way it's only the surface wave, which has formed as a result of a much deeper process. We can see the weaving and working of our own etheric organism during the course of our earthly life.' And he follows this with the remark that 'only the very small child, who hasn't yet learnt to speak, has the same relationship to the cosmos as someone who practises imagination in the proper manner. But this child hasn't yet separated out the power of thinking from the general (etheric) forces of growth.'[16]

Just to clarify our understanding of this passage, we should consider that for the person practising imagination, the transformation of our organism's life forces into the powers of thinking and willing, that Steiner described so often, no longer takes place. By entering into imagination through meditation (for this Steiner gave us the mantram 'in light flows living wisdom')[17] we can experience those life forces in which the small child existed before learning to speak and to think. These forces remain unconscious during our whole development and are active parallel to our conscious processes of perception, for they form our memory.[18]

In imaginative cognition this unconscious life part of memory enters consciousness not as separate memories but as the life tableau. In a certain way it performs a reverse transformation from the ordinary powers of thinking and ideas back into the life forces of the small child. Only then can the life tableau emerge with, at the same time, a review of how as a child our own soul formed our own physical body, our own aptitudes, but also our inhibitions, one-sidedness and attachments out of these life forces.

The life tableau thus reveals as an experience what the therapy approaches mentioned earlier always try to establish: the knowledge of how we were as small children and how we became the adults that we are in later life with all those talents but also all those inhibitions that we have.

As our soul works its way up through all the experiences of each level of the esoteric path and rises above the lower bodies, one after another, then we are able to perceive the next lowest body. The stages of higher cognition lead us in this way into the inner human being and at the same time into life before birth. In imagination we can look from the astral body into the etheric body in the form of the life tableau and see at the same time into the processes of early childhood, where our eternal human soul bound itself increasingly to the physical and etheric bodies. The life tableau allows us also to see the attachments and one-sidedness that belong to our incarnation—these are the causes of all suffering if we want to follow Buddhism.

For Steiner however the imaginative life tableau offers us human beings a starting point for higher levels of cognition, through which we can experience—in a Neoplatonic sense—the descent of our soul into earthly existence, allowing us to understand the immortal being of the soul.

If we look at all the descriptions Steiner gave of this in about twenty mainly public lectures in various places, of which I have compiled the most relevant extracts in this book, then we clearly get the impression that when we see the etheric formative forces of our own life story, this reveals to us those powers that have led to our becoming the person that we are today. As we get older this results in our appearing completely transparent in the life tableau and we can look at and work with much of what previously was baffling or incomprehensible to us.

The life tableau doesn't only give us an orientation in this respect, but helps the meditator find a connection to the time-form of their own existence. What does that mean? We can grasp the life tableau in a certain sense as the source of powers out of which our own life has formed itself. To unite consciously with this source means to be at one with oneself. We have found, so to speak, the source of our life. And precisely here lies the therapeutic value of the life tableau. If you have ever lost congruence with your life- and time-organism, for example through burn-out, you will know what it means not to be connected to your own life source.

The anthroposophic meditation movement needs to develop Steiner's teaching on the experience of the imaginative life tableau as the first result of meditative work and make its therapeutic dimension more accessible. For the imaginative view of our own life story makes it possible for us to achieve, in the form of a real higher state of consciousness, what many Eastern-oriented therapy approaches describe as mindfulness. Steiner's instructions suggest that through this imaginative work on our own biography, we can succeed in detaching ourselves from psychological entanglements, a goal of many of these spiritually-oriented therapy approaches, through a practical further development of everyday consciousness.

In almost all of his portrayals of the imaginative life tableau, Steiner follows up with a description of the next stage, inspirative cognition. To initiate inspiration, we must extinguish from our consciousness what we have previously imagined. Then, from behind the earthly life tableau, appears our supersensible soul being as we were before birth. Steiner emphasizes repeatedly that at this level we can attain real knowledge of life before birth and he challenges us to broaden our perspective and to add to the question of life after death, which is important to many people, the question of life before birth: immortality presupposes unbornness. Connected to this is the question of repeated earthly lives, which Steiner discusses in the context of the third level, that of intuitive cognition. I don't include any further such descriptions in this compilation.

On the whole it's remarkable, that in connection with the imaginative life tableau Steiner never speaks about experiencing our own karma, only about the overview in tableau form of our own life story between birth and death. Experiencing our own destiny and our repeated earthly lives only becomes possible at the stage of intuition. Interested readers can follow this by studying in full the lectures from which I have taken extracts here.

It's also striking that in none of his depictions of the imaginative life tableau and the subsequent inspirative insight into the soul's life before birth, does Steiner speak about the other side of this imaginative experience, namely the doppelgänger and Guardian of the Threshold described in detail in, for example, *How to Know Higher Worlds*. Also, in this context, there is never a mention of a threshold experience. Why that is remains an open question. Perhaps it is linked to the fact that the experience of the tableau is oriented towards life before birth and in this life before birth and in the child's first years of life, out of which the etheric forces and the life tableau form themselves, the Guardian of the Threshold doesn't appear.

In conclusion we must inquire about the possible connections between the imaginative life tableau described here as a result of meditation or, if you like, as a mystically oriented 'inner path' and the meditation linked to the observation of outer nature.[19] Steiner links mysticism as he understands it with observation of nature.[20] If the goal of the inwards directed exercises is to liberate consciousness which is bound to the physical (in the sense of the life tableau), then the goal of that meditation directed to the outside is the liberation of creation which is bound to nature. We as meditators can overcome this latter in its inertia by realizing the etheric, the life force in our thinking and our perception and thus restoring to nature her own true being. Self-knowledge and knowledge of nature meet where the inner path and the outer path flow into the etheric world.

In this respect both approaches can support and reinforce each other. If the outer path is typified by the observation of nature, supported by a revival of our own thinking in thought meditation, then the inner path seeks to strengthen the will through the retrospect and other will exercises, such as Steiner has often described.[21]

As far as method is concerned let me add that Steiner has described the esoteric path again and again and always shows new aspects, but he has never been systematic or even offered a manual on the subject. If you meditate in the anthroposophic sense today, you must yourself gather together the descriptions he gave in various contexts, which is a challenge in itself.

A methodically important stage preliminary to the life tableau experience are those retrospect exercises, which Steiner described in detail mainly before 1918, towards the end of the First World War, as an aid for the development of people's social skills.[22] The idea of these exercises is that we practise a 'selfless' review of our own lives in such a way that we observe ourselves as if from the outside and not going into our own inner life—and just there we find the difference to the psychotherapy approaches I mentioned before with their work with the 'inner child'.[23] But in the selfless life review we should regard those people who have supported or hindered our development, whereby Steiner emphasizes that the inhibiting influences are of greater importance—and this doesn't mean more *negative*[24] By letting these people 'appear in pictures', then according to Steiner, 'we gradually learn to forget ourselves, we discover that really almost all that we are we couldn't have become if this or that person hadn't intervened in our life in a supportive or an instructive manner.'[25] Through these exercises we can become more objective not least by 'objectifying' ourselves and thus freeing ourselves from the past and from past experiences: 'Objectifying yourself, freeing yourself in the present from the past, crystallizing the I out of its experiences, all this we must strive to do especially today as the present age tends to bind the I more and more to its experiences.'[26] Here Steiner defines perspectives and opportunities offered by spiritual science both for therapy and for our everyday life.

In this compilation of extracts from his lectures, Steiner doesn't go into detail about the meditation exercises leading to the life tableau. Only in the summary of the French course does he give a word meditation, which can lead to the imaginative experience of the life tableau. For readers who are not familiar with the anthroposophic path of meditation, I would point out that in this context Steiner refers his students again and again to his fundamental work on meditation and the esoteric path, *How to Know Higher Worlds*, whereby we must also include the supplementary exercises and the review exercises, which aren't explicitly mentioned there.[27]

The extracts compiled in this volume make up all the significant passages from Steiner's written work and from his lectures, in which he deals with the imaginative life tableau and the subsequent perception of life before birth. The lectures known as the French course, held in September 1922, which I have already mentioned and referenced, and the summary of the lecture cycle from the previous year in Christiania/Oslo, published under the title of *Three Steps to Anthroposophy* are central to this, as are the depictions in *The Spiritual Guidance of the Individual and Humanity*. Certain descriptions appear several times in the texts collected here, but the emphasis is always on a different aspect, so that the sequence of chapters builds one upon the other to provide an overview. The life tableau and the 'science of life before birth' arising from it, we can understand as complementary to the 'science of life after death', which has been studied widely in the anthroposophic movement. My aim with this compilation is to encourage people engaged in these questions to take an interest in and become more aware of the former.

Andreas Neider, 2017

Experiencing the Inner Child as the Starting Point for a New Philosophy

In the so-called French Course, held in September 1922 in Dornach, Rudolf Steiner describes meditation as a possibility to strengthen the power of thinking and speaks repeatedly of the life tableau as an expression of childhood forces.

If we want to attain imaginative knowledge in the right way, then when we meditate, we must have the whole image complex, to which we have surrendered ourselves with all the power of our soul, in front of us like, for example, a mathematical problem, so that no emotional idea or element of will influences the meditating. If you give yourself over to a mathematical problem, you know in each moment that with your whole soul activity you are absorbed in what is in front of your soul's eyes. You know that no emotions or feelings, no reminiscences from your past life should enter into what you are thinking and what should lead to a judgement about the problem in question. We must be in such a soul state to meditate in the right way.

Then it is best if you devote yourself to an image complex, which is completely new to you and where you know that you have certainly never thought this before. For if you just take up something from memory, then you cannot know what kinds of unconscious, emotional impulses are connected to it. Therefore, it is exceedingly good for the meditator if they can be advised by an experienced spiritual researcher, for such a person will take care that the meditator is given an imaginative content, which they can certainly never have thought about before, so that what they now meditate enters consciousness for the first time and that memories and instinctive reactions can play no part, so that only the soul-spiritual is involved in meditating.

Then if such a meditation, which need only be short on any one day, is continually repeated, then a soul state emerges, which lets the person feel quite clearly: now you live in an inner activity, which has freed itself from the physical body; now you live in an activity that is different from when you activate your thinking, your feeling or your will within the physical body. What confronts you here is that you can clearly feel that you are living in a world which is separate from the physical body. You are becoming accustomed to living in the etheric world and you can recognize this by the fact that your own organism, the physical organism, assumes a relatively objective character. In a certain sense you are looking at the physical organism from outside, just as you normally look from inside this same physical organism at external objects. But in inner experience what verifies the success of the meditation is that the thoughts become to some extent denser, they don't just have the same abstract character as they had before, but you experience something in the thoughts similar to the forces of growth, which have developed an adult human being out of a small child, or those forces which are active in you from day to day when your metabolism provides for your body.

Thinking takes on a real character. And exactly because thinking assumes a real character, so that you now feel yourself in thinking as you earlier felt yourself in the growth processes or the life processes, exactly for this reason, imaginative thinking must be attained by the method I have described. Because if you attain it in such a way that the unconscious, perhaps even the body, had played a part in the meditation, then those forces, those realities, which you now experience in supersensible thinking, these forces would in turn play back into the physical and into the etheric human organism. There they would unite with the forces of growth and the metabolic forces and by dwelling in such real thinking you would change your physical and your etheric organisms. On no account should this happen! All the activities, which you invest in this imaginative knowledge, all these forces must only be applied to the relationship of the human being to their environment. They should never be allowed to influence the physical or etheric organism. These last two must remain completely unchanged, so that when you acquire such faculties as being able to float, so to speak, with your thinking in the etheric world, you look back with your thinking at an unchanged physical body. The physical body has remained as it was; this etheric thinking does not influence it.

With this etheric thinking you feel yourself to be wholly outside your physical body, but you should always be able, through your own free will, to alternate this being outside with being wholly inside the physical organism. If you have achieved imaginative cognition through meditating in the right way, then you must be able to be in the one moment in this etheric thinking, which feels completely real like a growth process or a metabolic process, and in the next moment to leave this thinking, return to the physical body and see with your eyes as you normally see, hear with your ears as you normally hear and touch as you would normally do. You have to be able to bring about of your own free will this moving back and forth between being in the physical body and being outside it in the etheric. Then you have achieved the right imaginative cognition. [. . .]

If you want to become a spiritual researcher then it is essential that you practise various exercises over a long period of time and in a systematic manner. But in principle, through what I have indicated here, you will arrive at an experience of etheric thinking sufficient to allow you to at least make a judgement about the statements of a spiritual researcher, although this judgement can be made by the use of normal human common sense, if it is impartial and unbiased enough.

If meditation is to succeed in the right way then you must back it up with certain other soul exercises. Above all you have to develop more and more such soul characteristics as strength of character, inner truthfulness, a certain peace of mind and, most importantly, complete levelheadedness. This cannot be said too often: a levelheadedness that lets you practise the meditation exercises themselves, as well as all that you subsequently undertake towards exact clairvoyance, with a soul mood and a soul attitude as if you were studying a mathematical problem. If you develop as a matter of course such characteristics as strength of character, inner truthfulness, levelheadedness, a certain peace of mind, then if it is repeated again and again—for some people, according to their disposition, it takes a few weeks, for some it can take years—meditation is able to imprint its results on your whole physical and etheric human organism. Then you can attain an inner activity in imaginative cognition comparable to the activity of looking at the world through your senses and through your thinking in your physical body.

When someone has achieved such imaginative cognition,

they are able to look at their own life, the life they have lived through from childhood up to the present moment, in one piece as a tableau of the whole period. You have before you as your own life-story something which is constantly becoming, constantly moving in itself. But as you now regard this life-story through imaginative cognition, it's not similar to what you otherwise remember about your life; what you now see before you is just as real as those growth forces, life forces, which in the body of the small child drive the whole soul configuration, then the development of thinking and so on. Everything that develops inwardly, the development of the ether body in the course of a life, that is what you see. What you view here is much more real than that ordinary tableau of memories, which otherwise enters our normal consciousness and in comparison is only a kind of reflection, like a surface wave which is thrown up by deeper processes, into which you now penetrate; deeper life-processes, etheric processes, which don't normally enter our consciousness, but which shape us, form us and let us become what we are in life between birth and the present moment.

These facts, these processes appear before imaginative cognition. This gives you initially a real self-awareness of your earthly life. [. . .] With normal consciousness people cannot perceive this, because they haven't yet deepened their abstract thinking through meditation. If they deepen it through meditation, then they can perceive in a fully conscious state that interplay of the etheric human organism with the etheric in the cosmos, in which the small child, as yet undivided, lives. Therefore, I would like to utter the following paradoxical sentence: only they are real philosophers, who as mature people can still become little children in their souls. [. . .][28]

The exercises leading to inspiration, which I have described, are, for a more advanced super-sensible cognition, really only preliminary exercises. But through these exercises you can arrive at a perception of your own human life-story as I have characterized it and which, as etheric reality, lies behind the thinking, feeling and willing of human beings in the expanse of earthly existence. Then by removing those images, which you have attained in your consciousness either in meditation or as a consequence of meditation, by building up this empty consciousness, you can get to know the etheric beings of the cosmos and the spiritual beings weaving in these revelations. But if you become familiar in this way with human soul life, with human astral organisation, then it will become clear to you what exists as the legacy of inheritance in the physical body; or in other words what the human being inherits for the physical body from their ancestors in the continuing course of heredity. But you will also have an impression of what is not subject to heredity, but frees itself from heredity and is significant for the human individuality, of what therefore makes the human being in their etheric body and in their astral body free of what they have inherited from their forebears, from whom they receive their physical body. [. . .]

Please note: it is possible to do the exercises for removing soul content and for achieving an empty consciousness up to that point where the soul becomes so strong, that it can also abstract itself from its own life-story. And in this moment, when you are strong enough, then you live in a consciousness that no longer has the physical organism, no longer has the etheric organism in front of it, and thus no longer has the world in front of it, which is received through the physical and through the etheric organisms. For this consciousness the world of the senses with all its sense impressions is non-existent; for this consciousness all etheric events in the cosmos, which you have just reached through imaginative cognition, are also non-existent. You have therefore removed all of that. As a result, you have achieved the higher level of inspiration in your human soul. What then appears, through this higher level of inspiration in the human soul, is a state in which the soul existed in the soul-spiritual world before, through conception, through the life of the embryo, through birth, descending into a human physical organism. In this way you reach a contemplation of the pre-earthly existence of the human soul. You see into those worlds in which the soul existed before at conception it received, as it were, the first atom of its physical being. You look back at the development of this human soul in the soul-spiritual world, you get to know the pre-existent life of the human soul. Only now have you grasped one side of the eternalness of the human soul core. And when you have grasped that, only then have you essentially recognized the true nature of the human I-being, the spirit self. You can only find access to this if you have developed that inspiration, which can abstract not only from your own physical body and its impressions, but also from your own ether body as your life-story and its impressions.[29]

For ordinary consciousness, thoughts are usually experienced as thoughts about the external world of the senses, and thought memories, dull thoughts, which arise out of all kinds of emotional experiences and feelings. But now you will have a thinking, which, in the way I have already described, can take up into consciousness in active thoughts your own life-story, which you have lived through on earth from birth up until now. This concerns a deeper layer of your life-story. I have already said that it is not the memories, which we also have in our ordinary consciousness, but a deeper level. You can actually see into the etheric processes which build up the physical organism, which pervade and permeate it and have always permeated it. All that has happened since birth, all the growth that has been stimulated in the physical organism, all the various organs formed and developed, our thinking faculty, our feeling faculty and our faculty of will, all brought forth from the depths of our organisation, everything connected to real life which is otherwise concealed, all this shoots up in the form of active, substantial thoughts in an inner experience. You go, so to speak, from ordinary thinking, pass over an abyss and arrive at a thinking, which experiences your own etheric body.

When you discover imaginative cognition in this way, you must pay close attention to what, for those moments when you are in this imaginative cognition, falls away. The first thing you forget are actually the memories. You have memories in your ordinary consciousness, but next to ordinary consciousness this other, imaginative consciousness is developing. In this last there are no memories. To get an idea what this is like, I ask you to consider the following: even when you are remembering, as in all experiences in ordinary consciousness, you live really in the present. You perceive what you have in front of you at the present moment, you think thoughts about the present and when you remember past experiences, you have in that moment an image, which only points to the past. Hence ordinary consciousness experiences the present. Imaginative consciousness experiences the life-story in such a way, that the separate parts are seen all at once, as if those things that exist in time were like those that exist in space. [...] The events which you experienced in your thirtieth year, your eighteenth, your tenth, your seventh, your fifth year, they stand before your soul; they stand next to each other.[30]

The First Supersensible Experience: Time Becomes Space

When describing the imaginative life tableau, Rudolf Steiner repeatedly emphasizes that this is the first experience to which meditative work leads. You experience your own life-story not in a chronological way but as if it were spatial, all experiences simultaneously next to each other. Here we present the lecture from the previous chapter in the form of a written paper, in which Steiner gives a mantram appropriate to the task. It is particularly noteworthy how Steiner describes the process of meditation in relation to the growth forces of the small child.

It is best therefore if you choose as the content of your meditation something of which you can be sure that it is completely new for the soul. If you seek advice from an experienced spiritual researcher, they will take this most seriously. They will suggest a meditative content, which is simple and which you can have certainly never thought about before. It will not necessarily be a content which corresponds to something which you have already experienced, or even to anything in the sense-world. It could be an imaginary thought which doesn't correspond to any image in the outside world, for example: 'In light flows living wisdom'. What is important is to dwell on such an image complex. Through this dwelling on an image the soul-spiritual powers are strengthened, just as muscle power is strengthened through doing certain work. Any one meditation can be short, but it must be repeated over a long time, if it is to be successful. According to their disposition, this success can appear for one person after a few weeks, for another it may take years. If you want to become a spiritual researcher then you must practise such exercises in a strictly systematic and intense manner. Through meditating in the way shown here, you will first reach a stage of inner life where you can judge the statements of a spiritual researcher with more certainty than just through ordinary common sense. But if it is impartial and unbiased enough, the latter is also sufficient to make such a judgement.

Meditation must be supported by exercises for strength of character, inner truthfulness, tranquillity of soul life and complete levelheadedness. For only when the soul is permeated with these characteristics will it be able to imprint what develops in meditation onto the whole human organism.

If you are successful in this practice in the right way, then you will experience yourself in the etheric organism. The thought experience develops a new form. You experience thoughts not only in the abstract form as before, but in such a way that you can feel their inner strength. The thoughts you experienced before can only be thought; they don't have the power to become an activity. The thoughts you will now experience possess a power similar to the growth forces, which transform the small child into an adult. Precisely because of this, it is essential that you practise meditation in the right way. For if unconscious forces interfere in it, if it is not a purely soul-spiritual act carried out with complete levelheadedness, then impulses develop, which influence the human organism in a similar manner to the growth forces. On no account should this happen. Your own physical and etheric organism must remain completely unaffected by the meditation. With the right meditation you can, with the newly developed power of thought, begin to live *outside* your own physical and etheric organism. You experience the etheric; and you experience your own organism with a relative objectivity. You look at it and it reflects back in thought form what you experience in the etheric.

This experience is healthy if you attain a state in which you can alternate your own completely free will between existing in the etheric and existing in your physical body. If something is forcing you into the etheric existence, then it is not the right condition. You must be able to orientate yourself completely freely towards the inside or towards the outside of yourself.

The first experience you will attain through such inner work is the survey of your own past earthly life. You view this as it has become through the growth forces from childhood onwards. You view this as if in thought images which have condensed into growth forces. You don't have mere memory pictures of your own life. You have images of the actual etheric process, which took place in your own being without coming into ordinary consciousness. What lives in your consciousness and in your memory is only the abstract side effect of the real process. It is only a surface wave whose form is a result of a deeper process. You have a view of the workings of your own etheric body in the course of your life on earth.

Seeing this process reveals the working of the etheric cosmos on human beings. You can experience what is working there as the substance of philosophy. It is wisdom, not in the abstract form of concepts, but in the form of the workings of the ether in the cosmos.

For ordinary consciousness only the small child, which has not yet learnt to speak, is in the same relationship to the cosmos as someone engaged in imagination in the right way. But this child has not yet separated out the thought forces from the general (etheric) forces of growth. This only happens when it learns to speak. Then the abstract thought forces separate out of the pre-existing general growth forces. In later life humans have these abstract thought forces, but they are only in the physical organism, they are not gathered up into etheric existence. Therefore, humans cannot become conscious of their relationship to the ether. Someone who practises imagination is learning to do this.

The very small child is an unconscious philosopher; the philosopher practising imagination is again a small child, but awakened to full consciousness.[31]

This impressive portrayal is followed by a description of the level of inspiration:

Through the inspiration exercise you can add a new skill to those you have already developed: removing from your consciousness those images on which you have relied in meditation. I have to emphasize here, that you must develop the skill of removing *those* images, which you have previously taken up deliberately in your meditation, again out of your own free will. Removing images which were not taken into consciousness of your own free will is not enough. More soul energy is necessary to remove images which you have won in meditation than to erase ideas which have come into consciousness in another way. And it is this greater energy that you need to make progress in supersensible cognition.

In this way you can attain an alert, but quite empty soul life. You dwell in a wakeful consciousness. If you experience this state in complete levelheadedness, then the soul fills itself with spiritual facts, just as, through the senses, it fills itself with physical facts. That is the state of inspiration. You experience yourself with an inner life in the cosmos, just as you experience yourself with such an inner life in the physical organism. But you are aware that you are experiencing cosmic life in yourself, that spiritual things and cosmic processes are revealing themselves as your own inner soul life. However, the possibility must still be there to exchange of your own free will this inner experience of the cosmos for ordinary consciousness. Then you can always relate what you experience in inspiration to what you experience in ordinary consciousness. You can see in the cosmos you perceive with your senses an image of your spiritual experiences. This is similar to the process of comparing a new experience in life with an image which arises in consciousness from memory. The spiritual vision that you have gained is like the new experience, and the view of the cosmos through the senses is like the remembered image.

The spiritual vision of the cosmos which you gain in this way is different from the imaginative. In imaginative cognition general images emerge of etheric processes; in inspiration, images of spiritual beings emerge, who are active in these etheric processes. What you know in the physical world of the senses as sun and moon, as planets and constellations, you rediscover as cosmic beings. And your own soul-spiritual life appears embedded in the sphere of activity of these cosmic beings. Now we can understand the physical organism of human beings, because not only what we can see through our senses works in forming us and our lives, but also those beings who are actively creative in the realities of the world of the senses.[32]

In a later part of this paper Steiner returns to the subject of the life tableau and gives a more detailed description of how the experience of thinking is transformed. He clarifies not only the transition from thinking to 'non-thinking' but also the transition from ordinary memory to the life tableau. At the same time, he differentiates the tableau experience from visionary experience.

Through the exercises I have characterized above, thinking is the first faculty to be transformed by a higher consciousness. But you can't effect this transformation without having first lost your thinking. In a successful meditation you experience this loss of thinking. You feel your inner being, an indefinite inner experience takes place, but at first you can't experience yourself with such a strong sense of being, that you can capture this inwardness in thought form. This possibility only develops gradually. Inner activity increases and the power of thinking is ignited from a different side than in ordinary consciousness. In ordinary consciousness we experience ourselves only ever in the present moment. But by igniting thinking through these soul exercises, after we have been through non-thinking and have arrived at imagination, then we experience the content of our whole life-story from birth until the respective present moment as our own 'I'. Even the memories of ordinary consciousness are experiences of the present moment. They are images which we experience in the present and which through their content only indicate the past.

Such memories cease first when imagination begins. You behold the past as if it were the present. Just as in sense-perception you steer your awareness towards things which exist in space next to each other, so in imagination you steer the awakened activity of the soul towards the various events of your own life. You have the chronological sequence as a whole before you. All the content of your becoming appears present in this moment.

But in a higher consciousness you have something other than the memories of ordinary consciousness. You have before you the activity of the etheric organism, which was previously unknown to consciousness. The memories of ordinary consciousness are only images of what human beings have experienced through their physical organisms with the outside world. Imaginative consciousness however experiences the activity with which the etheric organism has worked on the physical organism.

When this experience emerges, you have the feeling that something is rising up out of the depths of your soul that had indeed already existed in your own being, but which had not sent up waves into consciousness. You must experience this in a completely levelheaded way. This is the case when ordinary consciousness is fully maintained next to imaginative consciousness. You must always be able to relate what you experience through the interplay of the etheric and the physical organism to the relevant memories of ordinary consciousness. If this is not possible then you are dealing not with an imagination but with a visionary experience.

In a visionary experience consciousness is not, as in imagination, filled with a new content in addition to the old, but is transformed; the old content cannot be brought to mind next to the new. Someone practising imagination has their ordinary person next to them; the visionary has transformed themselves into a completely different person.[33]

Steiner then returns to inspiration:

With inspiration a new element enters consciousness. You have to abstract yourself from your own life-story in the way I have described previously in order to achieve inspiration. But the power of activity which the soul has gained through imagination is preserved. In possession of this power the soul can attain an idea of what in the cosmos lies behind the etheric organism, just as the latter lies behind the physical.

And with this the soul is confronted with its own eternal being. In ordinary consciousness the soul can only actively develop ideas by taking hold of the physical body. The soul immerses itself in the physical body, which reflects back in images and ideas what the soul experiences with the etheric body. The soul does not experience the activity of the etheric body itself. Then in imaginative consciousness it experiences the etheric organism itself. However, this occurs through the fact that the soul has withdrawn its existence even further, namely into the astral organism. As long as the soul is only in imaginative cognition it is living unconsciously in the astral organism and looking at the etheric and physical organisms; once the soul is in inspired cognition then it is also looking at the astral organism. Because now the soul is living in its eternal core being. The soul can behold this by progressing towards intuitive cognition. Through intuitive cognition it lives in the spiritual world, just as it lives through the physical organism in ordinary existence.

In this way the soul realizes how the physical, etheric and astral organisms develop out of the spiritual world. But it can also observe the continual working of the spiritual on the organisation of the earthly 'human' being. It can see how the spiritual core of the human being immerses itself in the physical, etheric and astral organisms. This immersion is not as if the spiritual slips into a physical house, as if it lives inside it. No, it is the transformation of a part of the human soul into the physical and etheric organization. *This* part of the human soul *disappears* during earthly life by *transforming* itself into the physical and etheric organism.[34] It is that part of the soul which is experienced in reflection by ordinary consciousness through thinking. But the soul appears in another part of the human being. This is the case with that part of the soul's earthly existence which we experience as willing. Willing is different in character from thinking. In willing, even when awake in the ordinary sense, part of the human being is asleep. What you think stands clearly before your soul. In thinking, human beings are truly completely awake. In willing this is not the case. The will is stimulated by thoughts. As far as the thought goes is as far as the awakened consciousness goes. But then the act of will vanishes into the human organism. If I move my hand by my own will, in ordinary consciousness I have the thought which prompted it at the beginning and the sight of the hand raising with all the accompanying emotional soul experiences at the end of the working of the will. The middle remains unconscious. However, what happens in the depths of the organism, when your will is active in you, eludes your ordinary consciousness just as do your experiences when you are asleep. Even when they are awake a part of the human being is always asleep.

This is the part of the soul in which the soul-spiritual, that has not been transformed into the physical organism, lives on during earthly life. You can glimpse these relationships when, through the will exercises I have already described, you have attained true intuition. Then you can recognize behind willing, the eternal part of the human soul. This transforms itself into the organization of the head; it disappears into that form and existence during life on earth and then re-appears on the other side to go through death and to mature, so as to participate in a future physical earthly body and earthly life.[35]

Here it is very important to understand how the soul, in a way, 'divides itself up' in pre-birth existence. One part transforms itself into the formative forces of the etheric body and the physical body which develops out of these. We experience these forces as dead shadows in our thinking. The remaining part of the soul re-appears on 'the other side' as will. We can make both of these parts conscious through the thinking exercises, which lead to imagination, and through the will exercises, which Steiner doesn't expand on here and which lead to inspiration.[36]

Steiner now links his description of the imaginative life tableau to the philosophy of Bergson and his term for duration, in French 'durée', and relates this to the transformation of chronological experience into spatial experience, which he has described in detail.

The usual philosophy of ideas consists of thoughts; but there is no life in these thoughts, no substance. We obtain substance in imagination, when the physical organism falls away. Before this the thoughts of philosophy are only mirror images as I have described. If we develop a philosophy out of such thoughts, if we engage with them without prejudice, then we necessarily feel how unreal they are. Then we can sense that moment that I have characterized here as the moment when remembered thinking disappears completely. Augustine and Descartes sensed this moment too, but interpreted it inadequately as 'doubts'. But philosophy gains life when the entity of the life tableau emerges in the soul in a substantial way. Bergson sensed this and expressed it in his idea of 'duration'. But he didn't go any further.[37]

You've seen as well how, through that cognition, which leads to the experience of your own etheric body, you have before you your life-story as an entity; how what chronologically would be the events of your life-story stand next to each other. What you would usually see, one after another, you now realize, stand juxtaposed, as do things in space. Sensing this too, Bergson developed his idea of 'duration'. This idea of duration plays a large part in Bergson's philosophy; but in him it is just a hint of the truth. The truth is the imaginative view of time as in juxtaposition. Bergson only reaches the abstract sensing of the fact that, when we go more deeply into it, we go beyond this world now, but in the present, so that we experience duration itself. [. . .] Thus, Bergson manages only a reflected image of what, through imaginative cognition, we experience as events in time in juxtaposition, and he calls this experience of the reflective image duration, durée.[38]

Experiencing Life before Birth

In the French course, as well as in many other descriptions of the life tableau, Steiner emphasizes that the imaginative level of experience relates solely to earthly life from the present moment back to birth. Only with the subsequent removal of the life tableau, through the experience of inspiration, is our own higher being revealed to us, as we were before we descended through birth to life on earth. Then the real character of what we experience in a shadowy and lifeless way through thinking becomes evident: the higher origins of our thinking.

I have said already that there is a basic exercise for the development of inspirative cognition, in which the images that have emerged into consciousness in meditation or as a result of the meditation process are removed from consciousness. This however is really a preliminary exercise for another one. Through removing the images, we are able to view our own life story as I have described in my last talk. We are also able to see the spiritual cosmos in as far as it lives in etheric processes. We obtain an image of the living etheric cosmos projected onto the human being. We see how everything that we can count as heredity passes over from the physical organism of the ancestors to the physical organism of the descendants. But we can also see how a new force from the etheric cosmos is continually active in the reality of the etheric organism. *This* force is in opposition to heredity. It is a force which affects only the individual human being. It is particularly important for educators to understand this.

In order to make progress in supersensible cognition, you

must increasingly develop the exercise of banishing the imaginative pictures. The soul energy you need for the removal of the images will grow stronger. For initially you will only reach an overview of your life story since birth. You have before you a soul-spiritual aspect of the human being, but not such an aspect of which you could say it has existence beyond physical life.

Continuing these exercises for inspiration, you will discover that your strength in removing the images will grow. This strength will become so well-developed that you will be able to remove the whole panorama of the life tableau from consciousness. Then you will have a consciousness, free of all the contents of your own physical and etheric human being.

In this higher level of empty consciousness there appears through higher inspiration an image of your soul-spiritual being as it was before you entered the physical world and there united with the physical body, which formed through conception and embryonic development. You will gain insight into how the astral and the I organization clothe themselves in the etheric, which stems from the etheric cosmos, and in the physical, which develops through physical inheritance.

Only in this way will you achieve knowledge of the eternal inner core of human beings, which lives during earthly life in the reflection of the soul's thinking, feeling and willing. You will also get an idea of the true nature of thinking. This latter doesn't exist in its true form within the confines of earthly life.

Let us look at a human corpse. It has the form, the structure of a human being. Life has disappeared from it. If we understand the essence of a corpse then we don't think of it as something independent. We recognize it as the remains of a living, physical human being. The forces of external nature, to which the corpse is now exposed, can no doubt destroy it, but they cannot organize it or give it life. In a similar way, at a higher level of perception, we can recognize human earthly thinking as the defunct remains of what living thinking was, before we humans left the soul-spiritual world and entered life on earth. We cannot grasp the essence of thinking by studying its earthly manifestation, any more than we can understand the form of the human being from those forces which hold sway in a corpse. To recognize it *rightly* we have to view earthly thinking as a corpse.

If you are on the path to *such* an understanding, then you can comprehend the essence of earthly will. You can recognize it as being, in a certain sense, a younger part of the soul. What is behind willing has a similar relationship to thinking, as does the physical organism of a child to a dying old person. For the soul, however, childhood and old age, even a cadaver, don't develop *one after the other*, but exist *side by side.*

From what I have described we can discern certain consequences for a philosophy, which tries to develop its ideas exclusively out of life's experiences on earth. The only ideas available as content for such a philosophy will be either dead or at least dying. Therefore, the obligation of philosophy can only be to recognize the dead character of the world of thought and to come to the *conclusion* that dead thinking presupposes a previous living thinking. Insofar as we depend on the conceptual, evidence-based methodology of the physical human being, there can be no other possibility. This merely intellectualistic philosophy can therefore reach the true nature of the soul only indirectly. It can study the character of human thinking and recognize its dying nature. Then it can prove indirectly that the dead thinking presupposes something living, just as the corpse presupposes a living human being.

Only inspirative cognition can arrive at a real perception of the true soul being. Through the soul exercises for inspiration we can in a certain sense invigorate the corpse of thinking. We won't be transported back completely to that state before the beginning of earthly life, but we can enliven in ourselves a true image of that state, from whose essence we can recognize, that it radiates from a pre-earthly existence into earthly existence.[39]

The Three Levels of the Anthroposophical Path of Meditation

In his very first description of the imaginative life tableau in December 1920 during a public lecture in Basel, Steiner discussed the life tableau in some detail and linked it to the three levels of cognition of the anthroposophical path of meditation and its relationship to the three soul forces of thinking, feeling and willing.

I have reproduced the passage here in detail, so as to let the whole connection between the imaginative life tableau and the three levels of cognition of the spiritual path become clear. It is especially enlightening that Rudolf Steiner connects the depiction of the life tableau to a transformation of the forces of memory, whereas he connects the following level of inspiration to the higher development of the ability to love.

Spiritual science is based [. . .] on the fact that precisely because it acknowledges in a true sense the spirit of contemporary, natural scientific inquiry, it therefore accepts the limits determined by it within natural scientific research. It says that with those ordinary human abilities, as they have formed appropriate to contemporary human development, we can't help but stop at these boundaries. But these limits are not insurmountable. The human being is capable of developing beyond these perceptual boundaries. To begin with, I will draw your attention to two soul faculties, which are capable of higher development towards a particular supersensible path of cognition.

First of all I will indicate something which we all need as a fundamental force for a healthy life between birth and death:

this is human memory, the human ability to remember. From another point of view, I have referred to the special development of the capacity for memory through anthroposophical methods in the lectures on spiritual science. If something in this faculty of memory is not intact, then the whole inner human being is disrupted. If we feel that what we have experienced from that point in childhood onwards, when we could start remembering, has been interrupted, then in a way our I is not healthy. We feel disoriented in ourselves; we can't get our bearings in ourselves. In our souls we don't really know what to do with ourselves. During the course of our lives between birth and death, this faculty of memory preserves what we experience in this existence. What we experience in the moment gains permanence through the faculty of memory. Here we can apply one of the methodical aims of spiritual science by taking that force of the soul which gives rise to memory and then cultivating it in a manner very different from the way it would have developed if the soul were left to its own devices. What spiritual research uses here I have called in my writings meditation—an intimate process of the human soul.

But we really have to make ourselves aware of the fact that the paths leading into the supersensible worlds are intimate paths of the soul. [. . .] Meditation is such an intimate path of the soul. If you want me to describe this, I can do it briefly here; you will find it dealt with at length in my books, especially in *Occult Science* and in *How to Know Higher Worlds*. Briefly, I would like to characterize this meditation as follows: it consists of not just letting your thoughts follow each other out of what you observe in the external world or ordinary life, but through an effort of will bringing into the soul images or thought sequences, which you have either received from a skilful spiritual researcher or in some other way. Usually you think a thought as long as you perceive something or as long as your inner organization brings it up into memory and thus into your present soul life; in ordinary thought you more or less give yourself over to something involuntary. In meditation, however, you bring thoughts into your soul through a voluntary decision, through a real effort of will; and then you stay with them. You hold these thoughts in your soul. What I mean here is not something you can experience immediately; you need to practise this holding of thoughts for many years, if you want to achieve anything. I must emphasize that those methods, which only anthroposophy recommends, effectively hold the soul processes in a certain sphere. And you must be quite well prepared for this sphere, before you can develop appropriate spiritual scientific methods; you can prepare yourself well by conscientious training in modern natural scientific research. There you learn firstly to adhere closely to the objective facts, not to mix up random sympathies and antipathies with objective facts. And you also learn to follow the pure thought sequence, a certain logical succession of thoughts, whereby these thoughts themselves follow external observations. What you gain through being able to follow a thought logically is what can help you in these necessary preparations, for nothing should arise from the subconscious or the unconscious; the whole process must be as conscious and voluntary as the course of an experiment in the laboratory.

If you have managed to achieve such logical thinking, a thinking that the strictest mathematician could stand by, to use an expression of Goethe's, if you have attained this level of thinking and are able to dwell in the element of pure thinking, then you can raise certain thoughts into consciousness and—without the aid of memory, without the aid of external observation or anything else of an involuntary nature—you can hold them through your own effort of will. What are you really doing when you practise such an exercise again and again? You are continuing in the soul-spiritual realm the same process that took place involuntarily as you developed the faculty of memory. The child grows up and as it grows physically it simultaneously develops the faculty of memory. The spiritual researcher reproduces this ability to make thoughts durable, but in the soul-spiritual realm, by holding such thought elements in consciousness. Thus, you are really continuing this process, the process which has built up into the faculty of memory. And by steadily continuing this process, you will achieve a certain feeling, as if something is emerging that wasn't there before. Just as in a 15-year-old child inner forces are developing which didn't yet exist in the 10-year-old, so through such exercises inner powers develop in you that weren't there before. Before you only knew how to experience memory with the help of the physical body. Now you know how to live in the pure soul-spiritual realm based on this new experience with the exercise. You capture internally, in inner activity, the soul-spiritual and as a consequence the ordinary faculty of memory develops further into a special power, whose origins I will now describe.

For the spiritual researcher there comes a time when through such exercises ordinary memory is joined by something else, something that doesn't need memory, something in relation to which memory is no longer possible. From a certain point onwards through inner concentration, your life from birth, or at least from that moment where you start to remember, until now appears in images as a whole before you. It is as if time was no longer chronological but concurrent, simultaneous, so that the life tableau stands as a whole before the spiritual researcher.

Now something special has happened. The spiritual researcher can view as a whole what previously arose in them as separate individual memories and through this, they are confronted by a certain being—it is their own being, as they have developed since birth—which until then they had never encountered in this compact form. Before single memories had risen like waves from the sea, but now the sea itself has become, so to speak, visible as a whole. But then with our I we are outside this being that we normally are. Consider the significance of what is happening in the human soul. The human soul is ordinarily this being, out of which memories arise. Now consciousness remains completely intact, but our own being appears objectively, appears separated from us. Initially we have a general view of that being, which as a continuous being permeates us from birth to death. But someone who seriously wishes to devote themselves to spiritual research, must go further along this path that I have referred to as meditation.

Above all you must now develop another faculty, that already exists as a predisposition in the soul, but which you must develop in order to progress: the ability to love, to love the world and the beings of the world. It annoys many of our scientific contemporaries when we point this out. Let us look at love as it expresses itself in ordinary life. There, it is the devotion of one soul to another being, to a process or some such. What is love when it appears in our lives? We could say it is heightened attentiveness. Where is the beginning of love? It begins where, as the world passes by, I focus my attention on something. I single something out; I concentrate on this one thing. By concentrating on this one thing I allow the soul virtually to flow over into this thing, so that egoism recedes. As you become absorbed in the other being, out of your attentiveness flows love. We have to raise this love from a quality of everyday life to a real quality of cognition. We can achieve this by specifically augmenting the power of concentration, by becoming increasingly aware of the will, just as previously we had brought permanence into the life of thought. Before we had used the will in meditation, now we take care not only to meditate of our own free will, but to observe ourselves as we unfold our will. We look very closely at the will. We see how the will concentrates itself on something or other that we have brought into consciousness. And by heightening this inner soul activity—again it is an intimate, inner soul activity—we can now succeed in having a new inner experience. We achieve this by making ourselves conscious of something that is otherwise immersed in the twilight of the unconscious or the subconscious, namely the interconnection of waking and sleeping.

The human being goes through the world. From waking up until falling asleep consciousness unfolds and shows them the objects around them, which they can then work on internally through thinking. Then this consciousness is interrupted through the unconsciousness of sleep, where, at most, dream images arise. By having concentrated on the will and its development in this way, by having devoted our powers of concentration, devoted ourselves in love to something that we have taken into our consciousness, our inner soul lives have gradually gained strength, so that we know, if we put ourselves into a certain state, we can consciously repeat the same process that we otherwise go through when we fall asleep. And we know then, we know through direct perception: when I fall asleep, I go out of my physical body with my soul and spirit. From falling asleep until waking up I am a soul-spiritual being outside of my body. Before we have practised such exercises as I have described here, the state between falling asleep and waking up remains unconscious. This undifferentiated, at first completely unorganized soul-spiritual—which in normal life is only organized because it is in the body, taking form and inner strength from the body—this soul-spiritual, having gained strength as I have shown here, will become, through our own human inner activity, through meditation and concentration, as organized internally as otherwise only the body is organized. Just as the body with its sense organs can see in the world of the senses in which it lives, so will the soul-spiritual, if it has organized itself through inner strength, be able to leave the body consciously, as it does otherwise unconsciously when falling asleep. In turn it will be able to return consciously to the body, just as it does unconsciously when waking up. Now you get an idea of where we actually are between falling asleep and waking up; because you have awakened the soul to inner activity, you can obtain an impression of this soul life. Now, however, you have a different view of what previously appeared as a panorama of your life since birth.

By developing the soul-spiritual life through meditation, you will at first have an image retrospect of your life since birth, but you won't really know your way around this retrospect. It has indeed become objective, but you can't yet face it consciously. If you concentrate on working on the will, as I have described, then you will make yourself active enough to be able to hold outside the body what can normally only be outside the body during sleep. Then you can see in its true reality a process, which you couldn't otherwise see, because the forces that you needed to do so were not yet developed. Then you can see the process of the entering of the soul-spiritual into the physical body and the other process of the soul-spiritual being cast out of the physical body. If you succeed in understanding, consciously understanding, what falling asleep and waking up mean, then with this knowledge you will also be able to see and understand the meaning of being born and dying. Because just as the soul-spiritual, which begins to unfold itself each morning, is not born in that moment, neither does it die each time you go to sleep. Just as at birth or at conception the human soul-spiritual is not born in that moment, neither is it destroyed at death. You can determine this through real vision.

If through inner activity you get to know what really lies behind the human being, then you will learn to recognize it as that which transcends birth and death. Then you will learn to recognize it as what unites with the physical body at conception or at birth and in so doing organizes it, and as the soul-spiritual which unites in the same way with the physical body (although here not reorganizing but just, so to speak, improving the organization) as we wake up to again participate in life that continues in the morning with all its experiences. So you will learn to recognize that what really organizes the human being is what goes out of the body with death into the spiritual world. In this way by developing the vision of the soul, you learn to clearly see the eternal in the human being. We can't speculate or philosophize about the eternal—that will only ever end in sophistry. But if we can bring ourselves to inner activity, we can elucidate this eternal, which is otherwise unconscious, which lives for itself outside the body from falling asleep until waking up, we can recognize it as something eternal. When we have done this, we can at the same time recognize [what is otherwise unconscious] as something eternal.

This shows you how spiritual science understands the true higher development of the faculty of cognition. This is not about standing still and continuing only logically or experimentally, at the most more skilfully, but about really activating growth in our soul and spirit, new development just like the growth of the body itself, so that the soul-spiritual grows into the supersensible world and experiences the eternal. By experiencing the supersensible, by viewing life as if it were a day and realizing what went before this life and what follows it, then we will succeed in becoming completely absorbed in what we are concentrating on. Particularly when we try as well to eradicate the last vestiges of egoistic feeling from our concentration, then we can go so far as to be completely absorbed, but still retain the power to pull ourselves back. We shouldn't lose consciousness. Then we will get to know human beings in their essence, in the state of being outside the body. I have said that initially we learn to recognize life since birth in a kind of image retrospect. Then we learn to recognize what it is that becomes this life, that descends from the spiritual worlds into the body, that goes through the gates of death and returns to the spiritual world. But by becoming familiar with all this, we learn to recognize that ordinary ideas are not there in the eternal; the ideas we have in ordinary life are only produced in the physical organization.

It only becomes clear what the physical organization really is for us human beings when you can perceive the significance of external, bodily organization for the soul-spiritual. Only then do you realize that in order to form the ideas of the ordinary world, human beings have to return to their physical bodies. But we take the power of thinking, we take the faculty of forming ideas with us into the spiritual world and by developing a new thinking for a higher, supersensible consciousness, we can take from what is in our bodies a part, and I mean only a part, of our feeling and willing with us. But we cannot take ordinary thinking with us. We have to develop a completely new thinking for life outside the body. We can take a part of feeling with us from the ordinary life that we live between birth and death. But willing, in its true form, this willing is something extraordinarily dark, like something experienced in sleep; we only need to think of what ordinary counsellors and psychologists have to say about the will. Willing is a dark part of life. It becomes light when we raise ourselves up to true vision, but at the same time we have to recognize that it is connected to the eternal. Through loving concentration we can succeed in eliminating the last traces of egoistic, individual feeling that still keep us attached to the body, and also in developing pure feeling outside of the body, just as we have developed a new thinking in the pure soul-spiritual. But then we still have the will as it exists in the body. However, through the new feeling and the new thinking we can now learn to recognize it in such a way that we would perhaps have to call it desire. We get to know the will as desire, as a faculty of desire, as a force of desire. Outside the body it appears as the force of desire, but what is now the object of desire? The object of desire is life in the body itself. Now we can perceive the force through which we actually move from a life before birth to this life in the body.

We learn to recognize this desire as something that belongs to the world and which permeates us before we become earthly human beings and again stays with us when we go through the gates of death. And now we can see how this desire is something that acts in human beings and which has becoming human itself as the object of desire; now we see something remarkable, we see in ourselves the desire to become human per se. We get to know this life between death and birth; we recognize the eternal in it. We see on the other hand the desire to live a life and we discover the will as something from a human life that we ourselves have in earlier times lived and which has brought us into this present life; we get to know the will in its spiritual form.

If we look at the will itself, having extracted it from the physical body, then we learn to understand the fact of repeated earthly lives. Then we learn to see how the content of a life passes through the time between death and a new birth and develops in a purely spiritual way and how what develops in a purely spiritual way creates out of itself again and again the desire to become human. Through supersensible vision we can recognize, that the desire we develop here in life between birth and death and through which we desire external things, is just a weak reflection of those desires existing in us which carry us over from one earthly life to another. When we are in physical existence and desire one thing or another through our bodies, this now appears to us as just a weak reflection of what makes us human, what organizes the transition from one earthly life to the next.

I could only describe here in outline how, through an intimate development of our soul-spiritual lives, human beings can grow into the soul-spiritual world itself; how we first become aware of what we are between birth and death; how we become aware of our eternal being, which is beyond birth and death; how we also become aware that what lives in us between birth and death includes something eternal, which breaks out of this sheath and goes through death, but desires a new life. I would have to speak not for hours, but for weeks if I were to describe in detail what I have outlined here. I could describe it in detail, but here I wanted to show how anthroposophical spiritual science arrives at its findings and what conclusions it reaches. By developing our human cognitive faculty beyond ourselves, we attain knowledge of the essence of being human, of the eternal and of repeated earthly lives.[40]

Unbornness and Eternity

Interestingly it is in his public lectures in particular that Steiner describes in detail the imaginative life tableau. The following extract is taken from a lecture that he gave in April 1922 in The Hague and here Steiner explains how through the life tableau we can discover a 'second person' within us.

Just as a memory can arise out of my own being when I reflect on an experience in the outer world—if I only look at it I will have no memory of it later, only when I have thought about it—so through my having a thought and then having made it stronger in my soul, there can arise out of my own being something that at first resembles a memory, but which is not a memory. This is not a reminiscence of an experience in the external world of the senses, but something arising out of my inner life, that previously I had never noticed. If I may put it this way: just as memories arise from ordinary experiences, so through the power of intensified thinking there arises from inside me something that until now I have never inwardly seen. And very soon I will recognize what is rising up inside me. By making advances in meditation I try to achieve more and more clarity in what is coming up in me and then ultimately, I realize what it is. I realize: I am myself what is rising up in me, myself as I have become in the time since being born here on this earth.

Normally we only have the stream of memories out of which a single memory, which is otherwise down in the unconscious, will rise. These are not the memories I mean. These are the memories which arise in ordinary consciousness. But what is now emerging, summoned from the inner depths by the power of intensified thinking, this is not just a thought, a memory thought, this is something which leads me much more deeply into my inner human being than does the power of memory. This is something which effectively leads me down into deeper levels of my inner being than where the forces of memory lead me. This is what shows me how as a small child I employed faculties I had in my soul to mould and form my organism through the brain. This is what shows me how, as a slightly older child, I further developed my inner human being with the help of the faculty of speech. In short, my innermost life appears in front of my soul in a tremendous tableau, which I hadn't seen before. And what now appears before my soul is not just an image. Let me call your attention to this point. It is not just an image, but something which, when I understand it, I can recognize as something connected to my own forces of growth, with what grows in me, what lives in me in the forces of metabolism, in the forces of circulation and of breathing, what is actually my inner, supersensible body as opposed to the physical body. I now get to know a second person in me. I learn to be able to say the following to myself. You wear an outer body which spreads out into space, has arms, feet, a head and so on. That is a spatial body. But what you have now discovered through your meditation, through imaginative cognition, that is an organism which exists in time not in space, a time organism.

It is difficult for contemporary human beings, when we talk to them of such a time organism. But this time organism really exists in us as a second being and we are justified in calling it an organism. For when we have grown old, which I can definitely say of myself, we know we have a certain soul configuration. This soul configuration we now carry in ourselves is connected perhaps to a soul configuration in our fifth or sixth year of life. And so just as my left hand in my space organism is connected to some part of my brain in this same space organism, and as the brain is there in this space organism so that the individual parts are related to each other, so the individual parts of the time organism are related to each other. But in time, not in space. I carry this time organism within myself. In my books I have called it the ether body or body of formative forces. This body of formative forces is a time organism. It is the first thing we discover on the path of imaginative research. We have a survey of our life up to now, of its inner creative, supersensible forces. We don't speculate about a life force, but see our earthly life up to now as an internally organised tableau, as a time organism, as the body of formative forces.[41]

Later in this lecture, as in the French course, Steiner describes the exercises for inspiration, which consist of banishing the images we have developed in meditation from our consciousness, thereby creating a kind of 'empty consciousness'. In this 'empty consciousness' the soul-spiritual world, as we experienced it before birth and thus our real soul-spiritual being, then appears before us in the form of inspiration.

When now through empty consciousness a supersensible world emerges from our surroundings, then we are able to perceive more of ourselves than just the tableau form of the ether body I have already described. Now we are in a position to look beyond birth and conception. By being able to remove all that is the body of formative forces through empty consciousness we no longer see anything of the whole person between birth and the present moment of experience. For having learned to banish the imagination, to have empty consciousness, we can also banish all that lives in us as the ether body and then look back at ourselves with empty consciousness. For the person standing next to us our ordinary human being is still there, they can see us. But this heightened consciousness goes out into the world we were in before we descended from the soul-spiritual world and adopted an earthly body from our parents and grandparents. Now we see into the world in which we were united with those spiritual substances, which are in the spiritual world, before we were clothed in a physical body. Now we learn to recognize how we were before we descended into physical life. Now we learn to recognize something else through supersensible perception.

At first, by looking at ourselves as physical earthly beings, we have the physical body, the space body. Then we have the second body, which we can grasp through imaginative cognition and which is supersensible but does not lead beyond earthly life. And now we have the third body. As it leads us out into the world of the stars, we call it the astral body—this is only terminology. We recognize the actual human soul being. We recognize this third, the second supersensible body of human beings. We have this in our bodies in our earthly life, it clothes itself in the physical body. It existed before our birth, before our conception. Through perception we arrive at the knowledge of one side of the eternity of human beings. We have lost this one side of the eternity of human beings to such an extent that modern languages hardly have a word for it. We speak of immortality from what we know through tradition, but only through the tradition of the last millennia, we speak of the extension of life beyond death. To also be able to speak of an extension of life beyond birth would make it necessary for us to know something of the other side of eternity and to coin the word 'unbornness', as this unbornness is the other side of eternity.

Now in this way we have achieved knowledge, which could only gain access to our soul constitution through the fact that we got to know something which is hidden from our normal consciousness. I showed you how you must arrive at empty consciousness and how the content of the supersensible world comes into this empty consciousness from the spiritual world, just as ordinarily the content of the world of the senses enters through the eyes and ears. This second level of supersensible cognition I call inspiration: inspirative cognition. Through inspirative cognition we come directly into the actual supersensible world. Above all we learn to recognize ourselves as supersensible beings in our existence before birth.[42]

Pain and Sadness When Reliving the Life Tableau

In several lectures in Christiania in the year 1921 Rudolf Steiner spoke too about the remarkable survey of one's own life-story as the first result of imaginative experience. He also emphasizes that the life tableau facilitates a more profound self-knowledge and a deeper understanding of one's own being.

When you have had this inner experience, when you really feel that you no longer need to stay only in the world of the senses, that you experience something through your imaginative thinking, through your living thinking, when you have broken through the tapestry of the senses and try to look into your inner being, then you experience something that ordinary natural science doesn't experience, what ordinary mysticism can only bring before the soul in illusionary form. When you experience this honestly as the result of an inner development, then you can be sure that you are on a path which can really lead to higher worlds.

At first you have no external reality before you. You have only the old forces, strengthened and intensified. But very soon you will notice that in your human consciousness something essential, something important is happening. You will gradually experience something like an inner picture, which extends over your whole life from birth to the present moment. Yes, this is the first supersensible reality you experience: your own inner life since birth brought together in a tableau. And this tableau expresses itself in such a manner that your thinking will be different about what you now see as if from outside than it was towards what you then experienced in the outer world and how you inwardly reacted to it.

In ordinary life you develop thinking. You think about something. The thoughts are in the soul, they are subjective. The other is objective, the other is outside. You feel your thought activity as separate from what is outside. Now you have the tableau of your own life since birth in front of you, but the thoughts go into this fabric, so to speak. You feel as if you are in this fabric, a part of it. You say to yourself: now you are starting to really grasp yourself. You have to surrender your thoughts to what reveals itself objectively to your consciousness. At first this makes for a certain, I would say, painful experience for the anthroposophic spiritual researcher. The anthroposophic spiritual researcher has to go through such painful experiences in various aspects. You must not try to avoid undergoing inner difficulties, sometimes also pain. I will speak about this again today in a different context. Now though, you will at first experience through this life tableau, that you will find yourself in a kind of inner dejection. You won't feel the lightness with which you otherwise have thoughts, ideas, feelings, will impulses, desires and so on; you will feel them as something oppressive. In short, it is just in this oppressiveness that you feel reality. If you don't have this sadness then you have a thought edifice, but you don't yet have reality. By carrying into this sadness all that you had before as free developing thought, you are protected from developing with your imaginative cognition any kinds of illusions, visions or hallucinations [. . .]

Through what I have referred to above as reality, you will notice that what you have really grasped are not just thoughts but living forces, which have worked on building up our organism since we have been in earthly life. What reveals itself as imagination is none other than the sum of the forces through which we grow, the sum of the forces which work in our metabolism. Therefore, anthroposophic spiritual science calls the supersensible force that we discover in this way, the ether body or the body of formative forces. You see, in a completely systematic way you can discover a higher member of the human being, which at first works as a supersensible member on the shaping of our earthly life. And because you don't react as you do with ordinary thoughts when the life tableau appears before you, but in such a way that the sadness itself shows you the reality of it, you notice: what I am seeing within myself is the same as what is otherwise unconsciously at work in my organism.[43]

Here we learn in addition to previous descriptions, that the experience of one's own life story in the form of the imaginative life tableau can be quite painful, namely because we don't just view this historical development subjectively, but experience it as a force, a reality at work in the time organism.

We supplement this aspect with a short extract from a lecture from 1924, in which it becomes clear where the sadness of the life tableau comes from. It emerges namely that when we look at it imaginatively in depth, then the life tableau reveals all that we have neglected to do, all the consequences originating from such neglect or failure. We experience our own imperfection.

Now we have to continue with imaginative cognition. If we continue with imaginative cognition, then our lives are enriched and naturally we understand things accordingly in a different way than we have understood them before. Let us say, for example, that we are thinking about the way we treat other people, our behaviour towards other people. We consider what our intentions were with this behaviour and what we actually did, the manner in which we treated someone. In ordinary life we may perhaps think about such things in a particular situation, according to whether we are unreflecting or not; but now it is there. We have an idea of how we behave. But what we see there is really only one part of the matter. Let's assume we have done someone a good turn or a bad one. We would see positive results from the good deed, that the other person is pleased or satisfied—perhaps this has helped them in some way. We would see those consequences of our treatment of them which can manifest themselves in the physical world. If we have done something bad, we would be able to see how we have harmed the other person, how dissatisfied they were, possibly how they have suffered physically from it and so on. If we don't try to escape observing the consequences of our deed for the other person, if it is not too distressing, then we can observe all this within the boundaries of physical life.

But this is only one side of it. Every deed we do to someone else, even a deed that we do to the other kingdoms of nature, has another aspect. Let us assume you do someone a good deed. This good deed exists in the spiritual worlds and has a certain significance. It generates warmth so to speak in the spiritual worlds; it is like the source of radiating spiritual warmth. In the spiritual world soul warmth flows out from a good deed we have done someone. Soul coldness flows out from an evil deed we have done someone. And so we really carry soul warmth or soul coldness into the spiritual world according to how we behave towards other people. Other human deeds are such that they act like bright luminous beams in the spiritual world; others act like dark clouds in the spiritual world; in short, we can say that in our life on earth we actually only experience half of what we do.

Now if we practise imaginative consciousness, then what ordinary consciousness already knows fades in the light of this imaginative consciousness. To understand whether someone is helped or harmed is a matter for ordinary consciousness; but how a deed, whether good, evil, wise or foolish, affects the spiritual world as soul warmth, soul coldness, soul light or soul darkness and so on—a great variety is possible—this comes up before imaginative consciousness, this begins to be present. And we say to ourselves: just because you didn't know this as you let your ordinary consciousness guide your behaviour, doesn't mean it didn't exist. We say to ourselves: don't imagine that because you didn't know at the time that your deeds are the source of rays of light or warmth, just because you didn't see or experience this fact, don't imagine that it isn't there. Don't think that. You did experience it but in your subconscious. You went through all that. Just as your eyes, the soul eyes of your higher consciousness, now see it: if you have done a good deed and helped someone, if a bad deed and harmed someone, then parallel to that your subconscious experienced what the deed meant for the spiritual world.

And at that moment when someone has attained a level of imaginative consciousness that has intensified sufficiently, then they will not just look at a panorama of their experiences, but will necessarily have to realize that they are not a complete person, if they don't live through this other side of their behaviour, this other side of their earthly life, which they have previously neglected. We begin to feel quite handicapped with regard to this life panorama, which goes back to birth or before birth, as if something were missing. We keep saying to ourselves: you should have experienced this; you're like someone whose eye has been cut out or whose leg has been cut off; you're not a whole person. You've not actually had half of your experiences. It must necessarily come up in the course of imaginative consciousness, that we feel handicapped with regard to our experiences, that we feel above all how ordinary life blocks things out.[44]

After this explanatory passage, we return to the lecture in Christiania and to the aforementioned saddening and painful experience associated with the life tableau. Steiner then describes again the step towards inspirative cognition and explains how this can, in a sense, resolve those painful experiences.

As we have in the tableau only our own chronological life-story as a human being on the earth, we must continue on the path to supersensible worlds. We can achieve this through exercises, which further mobilize forces already slumbering in the soul. In human life there is not only remembering, the capacity for keeping hold of ideas, but also forgetting. Forgetting is, to our chagrin, often very easy in daily life. But someone who lives very much in their thoughts will know exactly how they can be a torment and how difficult it can be to suppress such thoughts. This can be especially difficult when we meditate in the systematic fashion I have described, when we develop deep inner thinking. When we focus on certain ideas and intensify the power of thinking, then these ideas are reluctant to leave. They oppress us. They only allow themselves to be suppressed when we practise it systematically. To express it paradoxically, we have to systematically through exercises train ourselves to forget, to suppress ideas, which want to remain.

[. . .] When we have practised such exercises in suppressing ideas for a while, we reach a level whereby we can empty our consciousness and still be wide awake. This is not as insignificant as you might think. Most people who lead an ordinary life will fall asleep sooner or later when they try to empty their consciousness. Now it is even more difficult to empty consciousness, when through meditation we have previously filled it with intensified ideas. But we must train ourselves to do it. And through practice we will slowly be able to suppress not only individual ideas, not only to remove them from our consciousness, but through constant effort we will become able to remove from our consciousness the whole tableau of life up to the present day, that I have talked about. This is almost the whole of our lives in a space which has become time, so to speak, or in time which has become space. It is the whole tableau of life up to now, which we have before us. Gradually, through the exercises I have suggested, we can develop the ability to banish this whole tableau from consciousness; first we have the tableau, then we empty our consciousness while still being awake.

This is an extremely important stage on the path to the reality of higher worlds. Because if we can arrive at being able to empty our consciousness completely, having first filled it with our life tableau, with the perception of our ether body, then we are not confronted with the void. We can in fact recognize that we are no longer surrounded by the world of the senses—the world of the senses is just as absent now as it is when we are in deep, dreamless sleep—but a world appears which we have not known until now, a world of supersensible beings and super-sensible events. We discover this world after having banished our own life tableau from our consciousness. It is just absurd, in the face of what then appears after all these efforts to say that these are only life reminiscences or illusions. If you really experience this, you know that you have reality before you—you know through direct experience, just as you recognize the reality of the world of the senses, that you have such a reality before you [. . .]

You have been through this or that in your life. What is in the past, what is no longer external reality, is in your memory as an image. Using this image, you can reconstruct the experience. It has, in a way, wandered into you from the external world and has become part of the content of your soul. From this soul content we construct at each moment the whole world of memory, the world of events in which we were involved. We seize the internal, we grasp it, we understand it in our life of thinking, feeling and willing. When we think about it the whole world of outer experience is conjured up before the soul. What, however, do we grasp through imagination and through inspiration?

We comprehend not only what we have experienced in earthly life but the whole human being. We learn to recognise how in all human organs the body of formative forces is at work and how it remains consistent throughout our lives. We learn to recognize how in a soul-spiritual world before conception and birth the astral body bears our eternal core being and how it enters us and works in us. The human being becomes, so to speak, completely transparent. We learn to recognize our physical being as the product of the spiritual. Just as by looking at our memories we can reconstruct our earthly life, so if we now look more deeply inside ourselves, if we look not only at what we have absorbed of the soul-spiritual during our earthly lives, then we can see how our organs are structured, how our etheric body, our astral body and our I are woven into this physical body. Just as memories lead us into the etheric body, similarly we can now see into the cosmic experience, world experience. For we as human beings were always present at all the developments of the world with which we are united, be they spiritual or soul events or on the physical plane. And if we can really behold ourselves in the way described here, through self-knowledge, then we can see how we developed as human beings through historical events, through cosmic events.[45]

And if you as a human being have attained inspirative cognition in the way I have described here and so can see into the world which you left at birth or at conception and which you will re-enter after death, then you will experience something which seems in its reflection in ordinary consciousness—and all supersensible experience appears somehow in ordinary consciousness as a vague feeling or something similar—like pessimism. What the spiritual researcher experiences through inspirative cognition seems like pessimism. Why pessimism? This is because when the spiritual researcher actually enters these higher worlds, he will experience something akin to a deep pain, an all-embracing feeling of deprivation. Now, through the exercises which I describe in my books, you should be prepared for this and able to valiantly endure this pain. But what is this pain? You will learn to recognize it as a reality. This pain is none other than the experience of the power with which the soul emerges out of the spiritual and into physical existence through birth and is really an intensive longing. Having lived in the spiritual worlds, the soul experiences the last period of time before descending into physical existence as a longing for the physical world. You will experience this longing as pain. And exactly the fact that you don't just have an abstract, theoretical experience through spiritual science, but that you are involved in spiritual science with your whole human being, with feeling and willing, constitutes the essence of this path into the higher worlds.

Theorizing is not enough to follow the anthroposophic path to the higher worlds. What you have to live through in following these methods of spiritual research demands moral preparation on all levels. And there is basically no better preparation for the moral strengthening of the whole human being, in body, soul and spirit, than those exercises which you must practise in order to attain awareness of the reality of supersensible worlds. They don't reveal themselves to mere theoreticians. They only reveal themselves to those who stake their whole humanity, who give themselves over completely to enlivening the powers of sensing and appreciating the world, of religious devotion to the mysteries of the universe and of developing love of humanity and of the world as forces of inner warmth. Only such a person can attain the moral strength necessary to enter into the reality of higher worlds. This is why some people point out that the exercises I have given for a spiritual scientific path to the higher worlds also have a moral aspect worth recognizing. This is also acknowledged by those who turn away, who don't follow the path leading to knowledge of the higher worlds. However, it is the only path which in the modern age as it is, with its longing for science, leads into these higher worlds.

By moving up through imagination and inspiration you arrive at first in your own self. However, this self has to surrender itself to the world around it. I have already explained how in imagination thinking has to flow out, so to speak, into the objective. We take this thinking with us everywhere. We take the whole level-headedness of thinking with us when we discover supersensible worlds. But we must become aware that our whole human being has to surrender, so to speak, to the reality of the supersensible worlds. After inspiration however, through the efforts we have made, through the experiences we have had, we can succeed in sensing the power of our I, the centre of our being. And here we can reach the point where we can recognize the harmony, the uniting of the experience of freedom with the experience of natural necessity. In normal life we are stuck in natural necessity. How strongly we can feel that, even when it has worked its way out of the worst of the sinful in the direction of the good, what lives in the impulses of our will still arises out of the instincts and natural urges in the unconscious depths of our soul lives. Just as we can consciously be as little aware of what we experience between falling asleep and waking up, so we can be unaware of what lives in the impulses of our will, which, in the end, contain much of what expresses itself in our conscious, responsible, moral life.

Someone who has been through imagination and inspiration however, will receive a strengthening of their I through the efforts they have made. They will experience their I more intensively. But they experience it in a sense in a surrendered way, flowing out to the world around them, though they experience it also as being given back to them. And now they are no longer able to say as a prejudiced, natural scientist would say: the same natural necessity with which the stone falls to the earth, the rock is warmed by the sun, which lives in electricity, in magnetism, in the acoustic and optical phenomena, this same necessity lives in me when I act as a human being, when I develop my will impulses as a human being. And in relation to these questions, ordinary science and ordinary life cannot get beyond scepticism.

On the one side stands human freedom, of which we are conscious. People believe they must deny this, if they are in any way honest scientific researchers, who believe in the conservation of energy and of mass. Consequently, they consider that no human will impulse, no human deed can originate from free will, because the human being is subject to natural necessity in common with all other beings and realms of nature. But if you now have your true I-being in a strengthened form before you, then you can attain a form of cognition which is higher even than inspiration and imagination. I have called this true intuition, true immersion in reality, spiritual reality. Here we get in a real sense to the heart of what anthroposophy calls repeated earthly lives. What appears as a necessity in our own deeds, our own will, reveals itself as the result of previous earthly lives.[46]

Here Steiner describes inspirative cognition in which we can experience our own unborn soul as longing for earthly life, a longing which the soul has just before birth. And we experience this longing in retrospect as pain. Here we can see the relationship between Steiner's concrete descriptions of the descent of the human soul out of life before birth into earthly existence and the philosophy of Neoplatonism or of Plotinus.

The pain of experiencing the longing before birth for earthly incarnation is a pain of deprivation, of being deprived of the real nature of the human soul, its innermost core being, which only becomes accessible through the third level of intuition, only touched on here. Intuition, this highest level of enhanced self-knowledge of the human soul described by Steiner, leads to the realization of repeated earthly lives, through which the immortal core of the human being develops.

Developing Courage and Will Power

After a renewed description of the insight you can attain into life before birth through inspirative consciousness, Steiner points out in the course of the lecture, that seeing your own life-story as an experience of the tableau can lead to developing moral strength, because looking at your own biography from the perspective of these forces creates courage. Through looking at the development of forces in our own lives, we can recognize those which have again and again led to progress and helped to overcome obstacles. Moreover, we must continue to develop our own will power.

If in the physical world we prefer to abide by observation and experiment, this is because it reassures us to a certain extent of the validity of our perceptions. We could argue epistemologically about the nature of sense perception and its relationship to true existence and so on, but that is not the point here. What's important here is that sense perception authenticates the validity of our soul experience, of what appears in the soul as a reflection of this sense perception, and we are reassured when we can rely on external reality. Recently even the disease of spiritualism has developed, which strives to confirm the existence of the spirit through external observation. Of course, no one is more of a materialist than a spiritualist. Spiritualism is only the potentiation of materialism, for they don't just assert that matter exists or even that only matter exists, but even that spirit itself should appear as matter, meaning spirit is nothing but matter. This spiritualism is the last phase, the ultimate consequence of materialism. True spiritual science aims to reach up into the spiritual worlds and not to drag the spiritual worlds down into material processes.

When, in the way I have described, we ascend into the spiritual worlds we no longer have the support of the external sense world for our soul experiences. We need a different support. We need something which reassures us in a way similar to external sense perception in the physical world that we are not floating in emptiness, that we are not experiencing just smoke and mirrors. And what we need there is something which we can only acquire through developing our inner faculties. Please understand me rightly. I don't mean that those faculties that we already have in ordinary life are sufficient—I just have to employ words borrowed from ordinary life. We have to develop powers in other areas than just thinking, so that we can achieve not just vision, but vision rooted in reality. What reassures us in the external world is that one sense supports the others. If there is a hearing sense impression or a visual one, it is still not certain whether or not it is a hallucination. It is only certain when the gravitation sense, so to speak, supports it, when another sense comes to our aid, when what we perceived through hearing or seeing isn't sufficiently validated through these sense perceptions alone, but is validated through another sense. So, what is it that makes us feel entitled to speak of reality in the physical world?

We can consider various aspects. I would have to speak on the theory of knowledge for hours—which I obviously can't do here—if I were to substantiate what I will now summarize. If you follow my train of thought you will see that the following is valid: in the world of the senses we call something real which appears to us in such a way that to deny it would be to deny our own reality. If you not only hear a bell ringing but can also touch it, relate it to its surroundings, you would have to annihilate yourself when you experience this reality internally in your soul, if you couldn't say this external thing were *real*. We call an external thing real when, if we didn't accept its reality, we would have to deny our own reality. You see, what we call reality depends intimately on our own reality. Therefore, we have to develop, out of our own soul, spiritual reality forces comparable to an object, which I can grasp and which makes itself known through its weight. We have to seek forces within ourselves to support the reality of the spiritual worlds, to which we can gain access as I have described. We can only do this if we develop further certain moral qualities, which we have in ordinary life thanks to our ethical behaviour. Just as we intensify the forces of thinking, so we have to intensify our moral forces. It's not just about developing these moral forces for the sake of our ethical life, but about strengthening them.

I would like to speak now only of two kinds. Firstly, we must intensify what we call moral courage, or what we call human courage in general, just as we have intensified the forces of thinking. We can intensify the courage that we already possess when we view in the right way, experience in the right way that tableau that we put before our souls as a retrospect in imaginative cognition. Then we will find that, when we immerse ourselves in our own lives, we will find a higher courage, a stronger inner power of courage than we need for external life, which we usually experience passively. This is the courage we have to intensify.

And we must strengthen another moral force. While courage is related to the life of feeling and represents a certain inner security, a certain inner strength, in relation to the will we must cultivate something which we can develop, when, for example, we firmly resolve to carry out a certain action at certain times and then with an iron will we bring about the conditions in which we can really do what we have decided to do. The anthroposophic spiritual researcher must also carry out such exercises systematically. We must connect the impulses of the will in the present to the impulses at the time of the decision. In ordinary life we give ourselves over to the present. In the life which will lead us to higher worlds we have to establish an inner continuity of will. We have to be able to focus our intention over years on doing something in a later time. Through this we can develop a strong will support, a strong stream of will which we have ourselves established. This is a very special form of self-discipline. We don't make ourselves dependent only on what our drives and instincts, or maybe even some ideal, urge us to do in the present moment for some outside reason; we connect a later point in time in the life of the soul to an earlier one in a soul-spiritual way through our will impulse. If we develop a higher form of courage in our soul, if we develop the continuity of will impulses, so that our will impulses last over time, then because we have ascended to the higher worlds as I have described, we can verify the reality of what we perceive, just as we otherwise do with regard to the external world of the senses. We must be able to verify this reality through having strengthened our inner faculties. Hence the path to higher worlds is not just a one-sided development of the power of cognition, but the development of the whole human being in thinking, feeling and willing, in the quest for knowledge, in an aesthetic and ethical striving. The path into these higher worlds is, at the same time, a religious immersion and a religious deepening of the human being.[47]

The Perspectival Alignment of the Life Tableau

The following is an extract from a further lecture in this public-lecture cycle in Christiania in which Steiner elaborates on the perspectivity of the life tableau. For as time appears in a sense spatial, a certain perspective is inherent in the vision of the life tableau and this leads us back to existence before birth.

[. . .] By moving backwards and forwards between supersensible vision and the ordinary state of consciousness we become increasingly capable of looking back, with those faculties we have developed in our feeling and our willing life, at what exists objectively outside the soul-spiritual core of the human being as the physical body and as the etheric body or body of formative forces. Having attained imaginative cognition we can really learn to recognize what we now have before us as an image from another world. And this is the important thing, that through imaginative and inspirative cognition, as described in the last few days, we learn to evaluate what we now see from the outside as the physical body and the etheric body. If I may use an analogy, it is as if someone has a picture before them and through their knowledge of perspective, they can recognize in this picture the corresponding reality it is supposed to represent. However, what we can recognize from an ordinary picture as the reality corresponding to it, is only an inner soul experience, while the perspective to which this objective physical body, this objective body of formative forces expand, when we have advanced in our spiritual development, is a factual experience. We learn namely to recognize that what is in this physical body, this body of formative forces, as an image, is the human being as they were before descending into the physical world through birth or conception. In a way, something frees itself from what we have before us, something that gives us a perspective back towards the soul-spiritual world, which we traversed before uniting ourselves through conception and birth with the physical matter we received through our parents and foreparents in the stream of physical heredity on the earth. And what our soul-spiritual surroundings were before we descended into earthly existence, the world in which those forces exist, which we integrated into the physical form bequeathed us by our parents and foreparents, opens up to us, to our vision.

Now we get to know ourselves in a state of pre-existence and the strange thing is that in this tableau showing the pre-existent human being we actually see the world basically in reverse in comparison with a physical perspective. In a physical perspective you see those things closest to you more clearly and then things that are further away become correspondingly less clear. This is the essence of perspective in the spatial world. But in the perspective that we now have, from the human being which has remained behind, it is reversed. For what is close to our physical earthly life, that is also close in present experience and we human beings do not know our own inner being during physical earthly life. It is our physical earthly life which obscures our eternal core being. However, when we look into the world of pre-existence what is closest doesn't become visible immediately, but what is further away becomes visible first. And when we have ascended through the three stages, which we can develop as higher levels of cognition through exercises, as I have described in my book,

How to Know Higher Worlds, then through imagination, inspiration and intuition we can attain a complete soul-spiritual world picture, which leads us back to a previous earthly life.

Just as a physical perspective has its limits in the distance, so a past earthly life, which reveals itself through intuition, forms the boundary of the image of the world we lived through in our pre-existent state. Anthroposophic spiritual science refers neither to phantasies nor to logical deductions when speaking of repeated earthly lives, but to what has been won through cognition, what has revealed itself to real spiritual vision. This spiritual vision must, however, be created out of the depths of our soul being. Then we can attain positive knowledge of the fact that those forces, which existed in the human being in the time between death and a new birth, have formed themselves into, have composed themselves into the human physical body and into the human etheric body or body of formative forces.

This also explains how we have developed out of the spiritual world into the physical world. And in the physical body, which we wear not only as a sheath but also as an instrument, and in the body of formative forces, which contains the vital forces forming the basis for the organs, for metabolism and for growth, into this physical body and etheric body, which appear objectively for spiritual vision, the core being of the soul, as it has developed in the soul-spiritual world since its last death until this birth, is crafted in. When we as feeling-thinking beings leave behind our physical and etheric bodies the last thing we recognize is what we turned to with longing before our birth, having grown old, so to speak, in life between death and a new birth and then having died in the spiritual world. Just as we find our physical bodies fading after a certain age, when we are old and approaching death, so we experience the fading of the soul-spiritual being, in which we exist in the spiritual world.

This fading expresses itself in a longing for the physical world, for physical incarnation in a body. And so, what lives in our physical body, in our etheric body, is in a certain sense the last phase of life above in the spiritual world. We leave our past behind us, when in sleep we go out of our physical body as feeling-willing beings. And what do we then take with us? By becoming clear that we leave our past behind us, we also become clear that what we experience, unconsciously for our ordinary consciousness, between falling asleep and waking up is that part of us which goes through the gates of death and returns to the soul-spiritual world. That part of the human being which couldn't immerse itself in the physical body and in the etheric body, which is left over, so to speak, this part goes out every night as we fall asleep and passes as a feeling-willing being through the gates of death again. Thus, eternity is validated for us through real vision.[48]

Intensive Backward Thinking

Steiner has perhaps characterized the life tableau in greatest detail in the lecture cycle in Christiania, so we include one last passage from there in which he again describes the tableau experience. He makes it clear that working on this tableau is easier for people who are in the second half of life. Working with the tableau is more suited to older people than to the young, because of the soul-spiritual development they go through during their lives. In this context he compares the imaginative life tableau to near-death experiences, in which such a life tableau also appears for a few moments, and so makes clear that the imaginative experience of the life tableau is similar to or even the same as the first situation a person faces directly after death.

But if we want to advance from the imaginative life tableau to the experience of life before birth, meaning the state from which our own earthly lives were formed, then we have to include some further exercises. One of these is well known as the retrospective exercise, in which in the evening we should look back at the experiences of the day as exactly as possible and in the reverse sequence. This visualizing backwards, which we can also practise with other chronological sequences, strengthens the power of thinking, which we need for the imaginative experience of the life tableau, and extends it through the practice of perceiving and visualizing in the opposite direction.

We can say that we human beings can experience nothing of the higher worlds but what we have cultivated in a serious struggle for knowledge. Through the intensifying of the power of thinking as I described yesterday, we must develop the possibility of consciously leaving our bodies and then being able to look back at them. We can only achieve this through intensifying the power of thinking. But we have to learn to discriminate: what we have from our previous life, we have through perception. What we will be in the future is only accessible to our inner experience. Therefore—as meagre as these inner experiences may be in comparison with what we have before us as a powerful, supersensible tableau from pre-existent life—this pre-existent life can become the actual content of a science we can now develop. What human beings learn about the future, however, will depend very much on this inner strengthening of their eternal feeling/willing being outside of their bodies. And you can observe this feeling/willing being in its development through physical earthly life and in its maturing towards a higher state after death. If you observe how what in ordinary life unconsciously leaves the body as you fall asleep, firstly in a more youthful state and then again in an older state, then you will notice a difference. What leaves the body of a younger person when they fall asleep, that contains more the thought life. It proves to be the thoughts which reverberate unconsciously in the younger person. When the person grows older, then they carry out of the physical body and through the gates of sleep into the outside world not so much the thought life as what lies in the forces of their character, in the forces of the will impulses they have developed. Therefore, we can say: we develop, in the course of earthly life, from a soul-spiritual being more filled with thoughts towards someone who has in their soul-spiritual being echoes of their character traits. Essentially, we don't go through the gates of sleep with our thoughts. We let go of thoughts as we fall asleep, they shine forth in the physical body. Those thoughts which filled our souls in earthly life between birth and death, we also leave behind there. We learn to see them as the external force of thought in the world; later after death we will learn to recognize them as an external world. We go through the gates of sleep with what has become our character, what has become our inner moral constitution. And if we really wish to interpret properly the phases of the perspective of pre-existent life, then we must acquire these powers of cognition through the further development of normal faculties of the soul.

In the last lecture I described how when a human being intensifies their thinking, their thought life through meditation, concentration of thought life, so that they can live in thoughts just as they otherwise live in sense images, so that their inner thought life becomes as strong, as alive, as intensive as their soul life is when they are immersed in sense impressions, then they will attain imaginative cognition. And through this inner thought life, which has intensified to the level of imaginative consciousness, you are now able to perceive not only the memory tableau of the life you have lived on earth up to this point, but you can see also all that the body of formative forces has wrought in this physical earth organism. You can see in a mighty tableau, as a first supersensible experience, the whole course of your own earthly life from this point back to childhood.

I mentioned in previous lectures that this tableau we experience is similar in a certain way to what appears when a person is in mortal danger that they will only just manage to survive. This has been studied enough for serious natural scientists to speak about it. For example, if someone is nearly drowning, then they experience in a great tableau the etheric body, the temporal body of formative forces—they see this body. This is the same thing that we see in supersensible cognition and it is the same thing we experience immediately after death, if we properly interpret the perspectivity of pre-existent life, that I have described. Here we can recognize that when a human being passes through the gates of death, then, for a short time—for about as long as a human being by virtue of their constitution is capable of going without sleep for several days—they receive a kind of tableau which lets them see their past earthly life as thoughts, but in images. We have such a survey of our earthly life for a short time when we have passed through the gates of death. I would say we have before us our life on earth as a kind of passive review without the involvement of feeling or willing and we get to know this state after death in the way I have described. First, we have to get to know it through supersensible cognition, through meditation and concentration and so on. But if we want to interpret rightly what connects this tableau of our past earthly life with life after death, then we need another kind of exercise.

In normal life and in ordinary science, human beings give themselves over with their thinking, their perceptions, their feelings and will impulses passively to the world outside. They move in step with the outside world. They experience yesterday and then, following it at a later time, today and then, in an even later time, tomorrow. And what they develop inwardly as thought reflections, feeling and will reflections in their soul lives, all this follows the external flow of life as a continuous, natural experience. In this process we have a kind of reinforcement for our ordinary thinking, our ordinary perception. But we can't strengthen our thinking to the degree that we need for supersensible research, if we only give ourselves up passively to the external run of the world. We have to practise other exercises; we have to try, if I can put it this way, to think backwards. This means that in the evening we can let the day pass through our soul in a kind of phantasy but in reverse order, from evening to morning—not in thoughts and not with any criticism, but in images, as if we would see again what we saw in the course of the day. We must acquire a certain practice in forming such imagery in reverse. It is relatively easy to imagine larger parts backwards, but you have to practise for a long time to be able to imagine smaller, almost micro parts in reverse, the whole progress of the day really back to front. Then we can move on to other exercises and help ourselves, for example, by going through a play from the fifth act backwards to the first act; or by following melodies inwardly from the end to the beginning, as if we hear them soul-spiritually. So we can arrive at a point where we can perceive our memories of life—and this is different from the described tableau—in such a way that we can really conjure up before our soul our whole life out of our memory, from the present moment on, all we have been through in reverse order and in visual images. By doing such exercises we free our thinking from external chronology. The habit of following external chronology with our thinking, with our perceiving, with our feeling, is deeply rooted; we have to overcome this habit. And through forceful backward thinking we become capable of accessing a much greater, stronger power of thinking than we need for merely passive thinking. Especially through backward thinking we can considerably strengthen the power of thinking.

And now we discover something that sounds paradoxical for ordinary consciousness, for ordinary perception. But just as we see the world of the senses with that thinking which flows along with the course of the world, so we can see the spiritual world, when we have freed our thinking from its fixation on external chronology. And we also gain another faculty. This gives us the possibility of observing the experiences following on from the life tableau, which we have for a few days after death, and of interpreting them rightly according to the perspective I have already described. Now we can see how then humans experience going backwards through their life in actual imagery in accordance with the life tableau. In a certain way they live through the soul world before the spiritual world. And they live from death back to birth faster than they have lived between birth and death. They live through their past life backwards. We can acquire the capacity to understand this by practising the exercises for backward thinking. And now we have an idea of how human beings experience all that they went through in earthly life in the physical body in reverse in their soul experience after death. But now they experience it in their soul and can see everything they did that affected their moral progress. In the course of this reverse time experience they can see from a higher perspective especially what they would now wish to be different. They can see how through their moral failings they have held themselves back in their development towards perfection. But as they experience all this vividly it is not a question of mere thoughts. In the life of the soul which runs backwards in this way, I could say develops backwards, thoughts don't remain abstract—we leave abstract thoughts behind us at death—they develop into thinking power. And they develop into the impulse to, in some way, make amends for those things which now confront the soul, in some way to do the opposite of what we did then.[49]

The perspective of life before birth and the difference between the imaginative perception of the life tableau and the inspirative experience of life before birth become again finer and clearer in an entry in a notebook that Steiner obviously wrote in preparation for the lecture from 29 November 1921, which we partly reproduced above. We should be aware however that these are just brief outlines in note form.

We recognize the structure of the human being—if we suppress this then inspirative cognition of life before birth emerges—then previous earthly lives—With life before birth = ether body attracted by the I and the astral body = these latter have already received their intrinsic character = the *astral body* is filled with the thoughts which it will incorporate into the ether body as formative forces—the *I* is filled with the power of concentration—which will be impressed upon the ether body—as well as later on the phys. body—

In the course of life, a person's feeling/willing being changes = it becomes more like the will, so that the person who before experienced more the fading echo of their thoughts—now experiences more the impulses of their character.

Through meditation and other exercises, the human being experiences death in images—the emancipation of the soul-spiritual = thus the perspective of life before birth.

Death in images: this is connected to the perspective of life before birth.[50]

The Life Tableau as the Second Level of Imaginative Perception

In the following lecture from September 1923 Steiner for once describes the life tableau as not being the first experience of imaginative vision in meditation, but that it only appears when the imaginative contents (of thinking) have been again removed from consciousness. In all other depictions he describes extinguishing the contents of consciousness as a second step after *the life tableau has appeared before the soul. Here, however, he describes imaginative practice as including the extinguishing of the subject matter of meditation, such as the mantram or an image or symbol you have meditated. Only then, according to Steiner, does the life tableau appear. The inspirative level then consists of extinguishing the life tableau itself. That it is perhaps a matter of practising this extinguishing twice is a new, possibly vital aspect of the life tableau. In addition, Steiner deals with another important aspect: learning to endure the life tableau because of the truth which it reveals about the development of our own being.*

If you practise this over a longer period, perhaps for years (you need patience and perseverance, for some it only takes a few weeks or months until there are signs of success, for others it takes years), then you can reach the point where you can apply this method to the inner organization of your thinking as accurately as a physicist or chemist utilizes the methods of weighing and measuring to learn the secrets of nature. You can apply what you have learnt through this practice to the further development of your thinking. Then at a certain point you will have a significant inner experience. There you will not only feel yourself to be in this thinking in images, which reproduces outside events and facts and which is basically all the more true the less it has its own character and is just an image, but you will be able to augment this thinking with your inner experience of living thinking, of empowered thinking. This is a significant experience. And I would say that through this, thinking starts to become something that you experience much as you would normally experience muscle power when you grasp an object or when you push against something. The experience of a reality which you have with regard to your breathing or your muscle activity, this inner activeness permeates your thinking. And because you have carefully studied each step along the way, you can experience this intensified active thinking with complete levelheadedness, with complete clarity. If people raise the objection that science must be based on experience and logic, then this is not valid here; for this experience is one of complete inner clarity and at the same time it is like a kind of feeling one's way in the soul. You feel your way forward by developing a thought, much as if putting out an antenna—not as a snail puts out an antenna in the physical world, but putting out a feeler into the spiritual world, which at this stage of your development exists more in an emotional way, but which you can rightly anticipate. Because you can say to yourself: your thinking has changed and has become a spiritual sensing. If this evolves then you can anticipate that this thinking will encounter something of a spiritual nature, just as here in the physical world your fingers will encounter things of a physical nature.

Only if you live for a while in this inner empowered thinking, do you have the possibility of achieving full self-knowledge. For then you know: through this concentration the soul has become a reality you can experience.

Now continuing with your practice, you come to the level where you can let go or remove the thought contents on which you have concentrated and which led to a real soul-sensing thinking. In a way, you empty your consciousness of what you yourself have brought into it. It is relatively easy to empty your consciousness in ordinary life: you only need to fall asleep. But you need a strong force to do this when you are used to concentrating on a particular thought content, especially with intensified thinking, with realized thinking, and then to send this content away. But just as first you obtained the power to concentrate, so now you can manage to remove the thought content. If you have managed that, then you will encounter in your soul something which you previously could only have in the form of episodic memory images. You are confronted in your soul by your whole inner life as a human being, as you have lived in this earthly existence from birth onwards or from that moment onwards when you began to remember, that moment when you consciously entered this earthly existence. Ordinarily all you know about your earthly existence is what you can recall from memory; you have pictures of your experiences. What you now experience through intensified thinking, however, is not the same thing. It appears in a mighty tableau, so that what you went through ten years ago for example is not just a pale image in your memory, but you experience it as if you went back in your mind through time. Let us say in your fiftieth year you do such an exercise which leads to this experience, then it will be as if time itself allows you to go back through a kind of 'time path' to experiences, for example, in your thirty-fifth year. You step back through time, you don't just feel a pale memory of what you experienced 15 years ago, you feel yourself immersed in it in all its vibrancy as if in the present. You step back in time, space loses its significance, time yields up a mighty memory tableau. This is a precise image of your life on earth. Even natural scientists admit that this happens in an episodic manner when people suffer a great shock, when they nearly drown, for example; then for a few moments they have some of their earthly life in images in their soul, which they think about later with a certain elation. In such a case this happens more or less as a force of nature, in our case, however, this actually appears before the soul as our whole earthly life spread out before us as a mighty but chronologically ordered spiritual tableau. Only now do we recognize ourselves, only now do we really have self-awareness.

We can easily distinguish this image of the inner human being from what is just a picture from memory. The memory picture shows how people, natural events or works of art come towards us from the outside; we have more the manner in which the world approaches us in these memory pictures. But in what appears as a supersensible memory tableau before us, we have coming towards us what actually emanates from us. For example, if we have started a friendship with someone we treasure at a certain point in our lives, then we encounter in images how this person approached us at a certain time, how they spoke to us, what we owe to them and so on. In the life tableau we encounter how we longed for this person and how we organized our lives so that we were in contact with this person we had recognized as a partner.

What has formed through our soul development confronts us with great clarity in the life tableau. Many people don't like such a degree of clarity, as it reveals too much about issues they would rather keep in the dark than have bathed in the light of truth. But we have to go through this and confront our own inner lives with complete impartiality, even when our inner selves reproach us for our scrutiny. I have called this level of cognition imaginative cognition or imagination.

Now we can continue from this level. What we have perceived in this life tableau are the inner forces which in reality have shaped us as human beings. Now, standing before this life tableau you know: in you those forces have developed, which worked on the substance of your physical body; in you, especially in your childhood, those forces have developed, which after your birth have organized and shaped the disordered brain-nerve-mass until your seventh year. At last we stop ascribing what forms and shapes us as human beings to forces attached to material substances. We stop doing that when we have the life tableau before us, when we see how the contents of this memory tableau flow into the forces of metabolism, respiration, and the circulation of the blood. The contents of the tableau are themselves forces, without which no blood would flow, no breath be drawn. Now we can recognize that humans are essentially soul-spiritual beings.

What we now begin to see we can characterize best with an analogy. Imagine you are walking across the ground, which is softened by rain, and everywhere there are tracks and furrows left by human feet and car wheels. Let's assume a being comes down from the moon and sees the condition of the ground but no people. Then this being would perhaps say: under the earth there must be all sorts of forces which have churned up these furrows and formed the earth in this way. Such a being could search *in* the earth for the forces which have caused these furrows. But someone who has understood what is happening knows that the earth hasn't made this, that human feet and car wheels have done it.

Someone who understands what is happening, as I have just described, will look with real respect at, for instance, the furrows of the human brain. But just as they know that the furrows in the ground don't come from forces in the earth itself, so they know now that these furrows in the brain don't come from material forces in the brain itself, but from the soul-spiritual nature of the human being, which we have now seen ourselves and which works in such a way that our brains have these furrows. This is the important thing: that we get to the point that we can recognize our own soul-spiritual being, that our inner eyes are really directed towards the soul-spiritual and how it appears in outside life.

And now we can go even further. After we have strengthened our inner self through concentrating on a certain thought content and then have emptied our consciousness, so that instead of the images we formed ourselves our own life content now appears before the soul, then we can remove the life tableau from consciousness just as before we removed a single idea, so that now consciousness is empty of it. Now we can learn to use a strong force to remove from consciousness what we first had to recognize through heightened self-observation as a soul-spiritual being. We remove in this process nothing less than our own inner soul life. We learnt to extinguish content from outside through concentration; then we learnt to direct our soul gaze towards our own soul-spiritual being, which then fills out the whole memory tableau. If we now succeed in extinguishing this memory tableau itself, then what I would really call 'empty' consciousness appears. Before we lived in the memory tableau or in what we ourselves chose to put before the soul; now something completely different emerges. We have suppressed what lives in ourselves and now expose ourselves with empty consciousness to the world. For the life of the soul this is something of extraordinary significance.[51]

Transforming the Forces of Memory

In the following lecture extract given to scientists and teachers of the first Waldorf school, Steiner speaks of imagination with a view to enhancing understanding of the laws of nature in a Goethean sense. Then, however, he describes the life tableau in depth and provides extraordinarily detailed instructions on how to work with it. It becomes clear that the imaginative life tableau is about transforming the forces of memory, whereas the subsequent inspiration is a matter of transforming forgetting. This power of forgetting has to be developed so that we are not restricted by the forces of memory from the life tableau.

This description makes us realize that the life tableau doesn't just appear of its own accord, but only slowly and after intensive meditative work. Furthermore it becomes clear that getting to know the life tableau also results in knowledge of one's own nerve-sense system, which is a completed system inasmuch as it appears from life before birth as if fully formed, whereas the rest of the organism is not fully formed at birth, but develops during the course of childhood and adolescence.

This lecture given at the beginning of 1921 in Stuttgart is, by the way, one of the earliest detailed descriptions of the life tableau experience as the first level of anthroposophic meditation.

Through imagination we gain an understanding not only of the world of the senses but also of the external world of plants. But we gain, as well, significant inner knowledge. To begin with I would like to speak of this inner knowledge in purely empirical terms. As human beings we are able to look back at what happened in our childhood from a certain year on during our waking life and we can pick out of this stream of experiences the one or the other event in image form. But we are clearly aware that in order to do this we have to make an effort with our faculty of memory, we have to pull up the separate images from the chronological flow of time. However, if we develop imaginative cognition more and more then we can eventually reach the point where time becomes quasi space. This happens only very gradually and you shouldn't think that results of something like imaginative cognition happen in one go. You shouldn't think that learning the imaginative method is any easier than learning the methods of the lab or the clinic or those of the planetarium and so on. They all need years of work, the one work on the mind, the other inner work on the soul. When we pick out an individual memory from the stream of our lives, we perceive time as flowing. However, as a result of our inner soul work the separate experiences merge together and we can see, in a way, how time becomes—at least approximately—space, and gathers together all that we have experienced in our lives from birth onwards into one significant memory image. Through the efforts of imaginative life this review, which is now more than just mere recollection, appears at certain moments before the soul. This is the subjective experience of the retrospect of our lives. It is, as I said, an empirical result of imaginative cognition.

What inner experience, or better, what kind of inner experience appears parallel to this vision, this panorama of our lives? What happens is this: we have these images of our experiences before us, but we are completely clear that the force in our souls, which confronts consciousness with these images, is closely related to our ordinary clear and bright intelligence. It is not this intelligence itself, but is closely related to it. We can confidently say that when we reach these memory images, we have achieved what we were striving for, namely that under all conditions we maintain a clear and lucid consciousness, just as we would do in mathematics. You have images but you hold them firmly just as you would hold the contents of your thinking. Through this you get an understanding of the workings of your intelligence; you have a vision of the significance of intelligence for you as a human being and for your own self-knowledge. You are not only looking back at your life, but this life reveals itself as if in a mirror, in such a way that we can really compare it to a mirror. Just as we can say of a mirror that by applying the laws of optics, we can recognize in their mirror images the objects reflected in it, so by achieving such inner vision we can recognize the effects of that soul force that we experience normally as intelligence. You experience, in a manner of speaking, intelligence intensified, an intelligence which is not only able to create abstract images but which can develop these very concrete pictures of your experiences.

However, something happens which constitutes a kind of subjective difficulty, but which we have only to understand in order to come to terms with it in the right way. You live in these images with complete mathematical clarity, but the sense of freedom—not freedom to do what we want but freedom of being—that you have in your intellect, you no longer have this in this form of imagination. Don't misunderstand me: the whole activity of imagining is as much an act of free will as is ordinary intellectual activity, but in intellectual activity you always have the subjective experience—I say experience because it is more than a sensation—that you are floating in the image, you are floating in something which is really, in comparison to the outside world, a 'nothing'. You don't have this feeling, this experience in relation to the content of the imaginative world; you have the experience that what you produce as imagination is at the same time really *there*, that you are living in something which really exists, that you are living and weaving in a reality, which may not exert a particularly strong hold on you, but whose hold you can nevertheless clearly feel.

And through what emerges from this reality, what we can gather from it by looking from the life panorama back to the inner activity which created this life panorama, there again we can recognize in inner mathematical mode that we can align it—just as we could align a mathematical idea with external physical/mineral reality—with what comprises human formative forces, what comprises the growth force in human beings (also true of the formative forces of other beings, but leaving that aside). We get an idea of a certain inner relationship between what lives purely in the soul in imaginative cognition, for it is purely a soul experience, and what weaves through the human being as the power of growth, which lets us grow from child to adult, which lets our limbs grow and which organizes our growth from inside us. In short, we have direct knowledge of what works in us as a real principle of growth. First, we get this insight in a certain area, namely the nervous system. Through experiencing the life panorama, as I have described, with all it entails, you first realize [. . .] what exists as the growth principle in the human nerve organism, which is an extension of the sense organism towards the inside. And you have the idea: you have in your sense organs something which you are beginning to understand through imagination. You now have the possibility of regarding the whole nerve organism as a nascent, synthesized sense organ, which encompasses the other sense organs. You learn to see that when we are born our senses are complete, not fully grown, but complete in their inner power—this is evident from what I have said about the relationship of imagination to the world of the senses. But what lives in our nerve organism and is permeated by the same force which permeates the sense organs, is something becoming, a great nascent sense organ. You will have this idea as a real vision, namely that we have the individual senses which open to the outside and continue on to the inside as the nerve organism, so that up until a certain age this nerve organism is organized by the same force that we have got to know, as I have described, in imaginative cognition.

Now you see what we are really after. We are trying to make transparent what is at first [. . .] spiritually opaque in human beings. What we can call soul-spiritually obscure, something that normal cognition cannot deal with, begins to become transparent in a soul-spiritual way. Now, with a kind of higher quality of mathematics, if I am allowed the term, we have the possibility of understanding first the world of the senses and then the world of our nerve organism. And now that we have arrived at such a level, we become not arrogant and immodest, but on the contrary, we begin to become rather humble in the face of our discoveries about being human. For what I have described here to you in relatively few words, this is something you can only acquire over a long period of time and although it develops in one person more quickly, in another more slowly, if you really practise the methods of spiritual science on yourself, we can still say: results which appear really fundamental and significant often surprise us after years of inner work. If we describe accurately enough what develops through such inner practice, it can sound perfectly reasonable to common sense. But to actually do it, to actually excavate such experiences from the depths of soul existence, this is something which needs sustained and forceful inner work on the soul. And this is why we learn to be modest, because we realize how hard we have to work to arrive at a relative degree of self-knowledge. For we see exactly what we achieve in imaginative cognition: you only get to know the human nerve-sense organism. And through this you now have an idea of the darkness before you in all that constitutes the rest of the human organism.

Then it is a question of reaching a higher level—the word 'higher' is just an expression—of supersensible cognition in order to progress beyond mere self-knowledge of the nerve-sense system. But here I must point out—I will talk about it later in greater detail—that achieving imaginative cognition essentially depends upon repeatedly putting before the soul clear and straightforward ideas, not in a confused way but in a methodically practised meditation, as I have described in my book, *How to Know Higher Worlds*. It is essential that these are clear and straightforward and not memories, reminiscences and so on—through such content we are all too easily seduced into surrendering mathematical clarity—and symbolic images are best, as these are most easily managed. It is important what we experience in our souls with these images. We try to place these images in our consciousness in such a way that they are like a memory image. Thus, we take images we have made ourselves into our consciousness voluntarily, just as we would take up a memory image. In a sense we imitate what happens in remembering. In remembering, certain experiences are rendered permanent as images. We try to understand what is going on in this activity of the human soul; how we do this I will explain later. In trying to discover what happens when we remember, we arrive at a point where we can voluntarily hold those images, clear ideas formed according to the pattern of memory, in our consciousness for relatively long periods of time. We grow able to extend this from a few seconds to several minutes. The images themselves are not important, but that, in holding these ideas we have ourselves chosen, we develop a certain inner power of the soul. Just as when we use our arms, the muscles develop through the effort we make, we strengthen certain soul forces when they have to deal with the images I have described, which we voluntarily bring into our consciousness again and again. The soul has to make an effort in order to do this and to hold the image, and it is this effort in the life of the soul which is important. By practising this, using self-made images, there begins to appear in us the power of imagination, which has developed according to the pattern of memory faculty, but which shouldn't be confused with this. And we will have to describe how what we perceive in imagination (we have partly described it already) are completely real, external phenomena and not, as in the images of memory, just our own experiences. This is basically the difference between imagination and the images of memory: the images of memory only reflect in pictures our own inner experiences, whereas imaginations, despite appearing like memory images, make it clear through their content, that they are not merely connected to our own experiences, but are related to objective phenomena in the world.

So you see, through developing the capacity of memory we can form the imaginative power of the soul. Now just as we can develop the power of memory, we can develop another faculty. It will perhaps seem strange to you when I name it. And yet developing this faculty is more difficult than developing memory. In ordinary life certain forces make for remembering but—and here, as colleagues, you will have to agree—also for forgetting, and sometimes we don't have to make a special effort to forget. This changes somewhat when we develop the intensified power of memory in meditation. Strange to say, this power of retaining certain images leads to them at first wanting to stay. When they appear in consciousness they are not so easily removed; they assert themselves. This is linked to what I just mentioned, that they are grounded in reality. This reality asserts itself by wanting to last. Having got to the point where using a mathematical model we have developed the power of imagination, now we have to make a renewed effort to banish these images from our consciousness, just as voluntarily as we put them there. And we have to cultivate especially this enhanced power of forgetting. It is very important when developing these inner powers of cognition, that you really take great care not to cause harm to the soul. But someone who only points out the dangers is like someone who would prohibit certain experiments in the lab because something could explode. You see, I myself had a chemistry professor at university, who only had one eye because he lost the other one during an experiment. Of course, something like that can't be used as an objection to developing certain methods and I must say that if you observe all the safety precautions I have given in my books with regard to developing inner soul forces, then your soul won't be in any danger. If you don't develop the method of getting rid of the images, then you run the risk of being shackled to those you have developed in your meditation. This shouldn't be allowed to happen and would lead to stagnation on the path of supersensible knowledge. Hence the next level of development is the process of enhanced forgetting. Now there is a certain resource that we can use to achieve this level of enhanced forgetting. I'm coming to something which to those who are involved in any way with the modern theory of knowledge will seem amateurish. I'm aware of all the objections which can be raised against something like this, but I am duty-bound to state the facts as they are. And so, I have to say that you can come to your own aid in strengthening forgetting, if through self-discipline, the discipline of your own self, you develop what appears in ordinary life as the capacity for love. Sure enough, you can say: love is not a power of cognition. In the manner that cognition is understood today this is probably true. But it is not a case of retaining the capacity for love as it exists in and for ordinary life, but of developing this capacity for love through a certain self-discipline. And you can achieve this by observing the following.

Isn't it true that in the course of our human lives, we have to admit that with each year that passes we become in some way a different person? And if we compare what we are in a certain year with what we were ten years ago, then, if we are honest with ourselves, we will find that what is the substance of our soul life, not just the content of our thinking life or our feelings or will, but is characteristic of our whole soul constitution, that this has changed in some ways over time. We have become different people inside and when we look at what has caused this change, we can say in the first instance it is what has happened to the physical organism, which is always changing. In the first half of our lives it changes through constant growth; in the second half of life it changes through the decline of the body and so on. But also, external events that confront us as the world of ideas, all that causes us pain, desire or joy in our soul and also the willpower we have tried to develop and express, all this is what makes us into someone else over the course of our lives. And if we want to be honest with ourselves on this point we have to say: we have just gone with the flow of our lives. But if you want to become a spiritual researcher then you must yourself take charge of your own development through self-discipline. You have to educate yourself by resolving that within a certain period you will transform a habit—sometimes the smaller habits are the crucial ones—through your own activity, so that you metamorphose yourself in the course of your life. Not only the flow of life itself but also the work you have in full consciousness done on yourself, allows you then to look back from some point in your life with the help of the retrospective life panorama you have already developed and to see what has changed through your own self-discipline. This in turn then affects your soul life in a remarkable way. It affects your soul life not in the sense of heightening egoism, but just the opposite, in the sense of enhancing your capacity for love. You will become more and more capable of embracing the outside world, of immersing yourself in the outside world to a certain degree with love. And only someone who has practised this self-discipline intensively can really form an opinion of what this means. Only such a person can appreciate the significance of tempering the thoughts we form of some object or of some event with the results of such self-discipline. Then we are much more deeply personally involved in what our thoughts are engaged with, we are even more deeply involved with a certain degree of love in the physical-mineral realm, which with only our mathematical thinking would otherwise leave us cold. We perceive very clearly the difference between our involvement in the world with only our weak power of thought and of being involved in it with the enhanced power of love.

You will only take offence at what I have said here about the enhanced power of love if you want to establish the dogma that this power of love has no place in cognition of the outside world. Yes, you could assert this dogma. You could say that we can only attain exact, objective knowledge through purely logical cognition. Certainly, we need that capacity, which by excluding all other forces but the sober power of reason can observe the events of the external world. But the outside world doesn't yield itself up completely to this form of involvement; the world only yields itself up completely to us when we involve ourselves in it with the enhanced power of love. And it's not a question of commanding knowledge, of saying nature must open itself to us in this way or that, of asserting epistemological dogmas, but of asking: how does nature become accessible to us? How does nature open up to us? Nature only opens up to us when we permeate our cognitive forces with the power of love.

For now, however, I'm only talking about trying to develop the exercises of forgetting, which will be stronger and more reliable with the power of love than without it. At the same time practising self-discipline, which makes us more capable of love, we can get to a point where we can actually experience enhanced forgetting just as voluntarily as we experienced enhanced remembering. And we put something specific, something positive in our souls at that point where normally we are at the end of the experience—because when we have forgotten something that is usually the end of a certain series of events. In the place where there is usually nothing, we put something positive—enhanced forgetting, whereby we actively develop something which usually just happens passively. When we have achieved this, it is as if we have crossed an inner abyss, as if we have actually entered a region of experience which brings us a new existence. And it is so. Up until now we have had our imaginations. If we are really well-prepared with our mathematical soul-attitude in these imaginations and not just fools, then we will see clearly: in the imaginative world we have images. Physiologists may dispute whether what our senses communicate are images of reality or reality itself—I have discussed this in my *Riddles of Philosophy*. That they are first of all images, which are no doubt an indication of reality, this we know and it is exactly this which constitutes a healthy experience in such a region, in knowing that we are dealing with images. As a certain result of enhanced forgetting however, there comes a point at which these images fill with spiritual reality from the other side of life so to speak, and then we merge with spiritual reality. We perceive, as it were, the other end of life. Just as through our senses we perceive the one end of life, namely the physical sense-world, so we learn to look into the other side and we learn to perceive how spiritual reality flows into the pictures of imaginative life. This flowing in of spiritual reality at the edge of the abyss of soul existence into what we have prepared within our faculty of cognition I have called inspiration in my book, *How to Know Higher Worlds* and in other books. You don't need to get caught up in the expression, you just need to hold on to what is meant by the essence of such words. Don't get caught up in recollections of where you have heard the word before. We need words for what we are trying to communicate and often have to use older words and so I have chosen, for what develops as I have described, the word inspiration.[52]

Feelings of Happiness When Experiencing the Life Tableau

There now follows a description of the life tableau, which Steiner gave in a summer course on 'Initiation Knowledge' in Wales in 1923. Here too he describes the experience of the life tableau as one of the first steps in imaginative cognition. He discusses in detail the feelings of happiness which accompany the experience of the life tableau. He also describes the two-dimensional quality of imaginative experience. Then, describing the next step towards inspirative cognition, following the life tableau, Steiner again emphasizes the necessity of taking life before birth as seriously as life after death, and he calls upon us to speak not only of immortality but also of 'unbornness'.

Now, the first experience you have in this way will be true human self-knowledge. Just as at this moment we perceive the existence of the table, the chairs, the whole lovely hall here, the clock which has stopped and so on, just as this all stands before us in our experience of the outside world and constitutes a perception in the present moment, so too does the world of time stand before our realized thinking, our intensified thinking, the world of time of our own human self. What we have experienced and what we can usually only draw out of our memory and into consciousness as an image, this becomes a tableau in the present, in which what is long past becomes present. People who are in shock from a life-threatening situation they have been through, such as nearly drowning, describe the same thing, and even people who are wholly materialistic in their thinking—I always emphasize this—accept that those concerned, experience a tableau of their own earthly life. For someone who has activated their thinking in this way, a tableau appears before their soul, which extends from the time when they learnt to think up until the present moment all in one piece. Time becomes space. What is past becomes present. An image appears. Typically, and I will speak more of this tomorrow, because it is an image you will have a sense of space, but only a *sense* of space, as this space you now experience is missing the third dimension. You experience no third dimension, just everywhere space in only two dimensions; so, you experience an image. This is why I call it imaginative cognition, because it works, as does painting, in two dimensions and so it is an image cognition, a cognition which extends only in two dimensions.

You could raise the question: when I stand there and experience two dimensions, what happens when I go forward and then experience two dimensions again?

There is no difference between the two. As an experience the third dimension is missing completely. Later on, I will have to speak about the fact that, because there is no longer any awareness of these things in our times, people seek the fourth dimension in order to enter the spiritual world. The truth is that as soon as you go from the physical to the spiritual, there doesn't appear a fourth dimension, but the third dimension falls away. We have to get used to reality in this field as we have had to get used to reality in other fields. People used to believe that the earth is flat and that you would arrive at the end of the world, which is boarded up. But then there was progress as people realized, if you go on far enough you arrive back at your starting point. So, there will be progress in our inner understanding of the world, when people realize that you don't advance from the first, the second and third dimension into the fourth dimension when you enter the spiritual, but rather you go back to the second dimension. And we will see how, later, you even go back to the first dimension. This is the truth. It becomes clear that in the contemporary, outward view of the world people approach the question in a completely external, I'd like to say numerative way: first dimension, second dimension, third dimension—there must be a fourth dimension. No, you return to the second dimension, the third cancels itself out and you get real imaginative cognition, which at first appears in your own self as a life tableau. You have an overview in the present moment in mighty images—I will speak more about this later—of what you have gone through in your earthly life, of your inner experience of this earthly life.

There is a great difference between this and mere memories. Ordinary memories appear in such a way that we have the feeling that they mainly consist of our perceptions of the outside world, what we have experienced as pleasant or painful, what others did to us, how other people related to us. This is how we generally experience our memories, which consist of mere pictures. In this tableau I'm speaking of, you have a different experience. In mere memory—let's say you met someone ten years ago—you remember how they approached you, how they treated you, well or badly, and so on. In this life tableau, however, you experience how you yourself turned your attention towards this person, what you did, what you went through to get them to like you, what you felt. You experience in this life tableau what flowed from inside towards the world, whereas memory only gives you what flowed from outside towards you.

So you could say that this life tableau is an experience in

the immediate present, in which, unlike memory, where things happen one after the other, everything stands in two-dimensional space adjacent to each other. You can easily differentiate the life tableau from an ordinary memory tableau.

Now what you have achieved in doing this is that you have increased your inner activity, your active experience of your own personality. This is the essential thing. You live more intensively; you develop those forces which originate in your personality more intensively. When you have got this far you must then go on to the next step. Nobody likes to take this step. And I have to allow that it will cost you considerable effort. Because in the experience of the tableau, in these images, where these experiences appear before the soul, even those which were painful when you went through them in the past, what you have is a subjective feeling of happiness. Connected to this imaginative cognition is a tremendously strong, subjective feeling of happiness.

All those religious ideals and descriptions, as, for example, in Islam, which conceive of existence beyond earthly life in images of joy and delight, have originated in this feeling of subjective happiness.

If you want to take the next step, you must forget these feelings of happiness. For having, through meditation, concentration and thinking, voluntarily enhanced that thinking as I have described, and then through this enhanced thinking having arrived at the tableau of your own life, it is now necessary to do your utmost to banish all that out of your consciousness.

Getting rid of the contents of our consciousness is sometimes quite easy in ordinary life. People who are taking exams can tell you a thing or two about emptying their consciousness of its contents, when really it should be full. And normal sleep is actually just the removing of the content of everyday consciousness. But this too happens passively, for someone taking an exam wouldn't voluntarily extinguish what they know. Human beings do this out of weakness, out of the weakness of the force of modern consciousness. However, having just strengthened this force, then we have to turn it off in order to take the next step on the path of supersensible cognition.

Now it can very easily happen that having concentrated all our soul powers on such a self-chosen content we now have a certain tendency to stick to it and because of the feeling of happiness associated with the life tableau, we like to linger there. We want to hold onto it. But now we have to be able to eliminate from our consciousness all that we have struggled to attain through a kind of intensification of our soul forces. It is more difficult than forgetting in ordinary life, as I have mentioned.

You will be aware that if you gradually deprive a human being of sense impressions, if you make a room so dark that they can see nothing, if you make everything quiet so they can hear nothing and then you suppress even touch, then that person will fall asleep. This empty consciousness where you normally fall asleep, this is what you bring about voluntarily. But even though you have removed all impressions on your consciousness, even self-made ones, you must still be awake. This is the important thing, just being awake, the power, the inner activity of being awake but with no external impressions, no more self-made experiences. This is creating empty consciousness, but fully experienced empty consciousness.

Then when you have removed what you had just brought into your consciousness through enhanced soul power, when you create empty consciousness, this consciousness does not remain empty. Then you reach the second level of cognition, which as opposed to imaginative cognition we can call inspirative cognition. When we have attained such an empty consciousness, then it becomes possible that, just as for the eye the visible world, [for the ear] the audible world appears, so now the spiritual world appears before our souls. Now it is no longer our own experience, it is the external spiritual world which permeates us and appears before us. And if we are strong enough to not only eliminate parts of the life tableau we have developed, but to eliminate the whole life tableau at once, so that we can let it come, then remove it again, so that having had the life tableau we now have empty consciousness, but are still awake—then, in turn, the first thing that enters this empty consciousness is our life before birth, that life we had before we descended through conception into an earthly body. This is the first real supersensible experience we go through after having created empty consciousness: we see our own life before birth. From this moment on we know the immortality of human beings from an aspect which these days is never mentioned. Today we only speak of immortality. We don't learn about reality. Immortality is the negation of death. This is certainly as true as the other aspect—there will be much to say about this—but what we get to know at first on the path of cognition, which I could only sketch out today, that is not immortality, negation of death, that is 'unbornness', the negation of birth. Unbornness is as essential to humanity as immortality. And when we again understand that eternity has these two aspects, immortality and unbornness, then we will be able to recognize cognitively what is everlasting, the true eternal aspect of the human being.

The newer languages all still have a word for immortality, but they have lost the word unbornness, which the old languages all had. First, we lost the one aspect of eternity, unbornness, and now, in the age of materialism, humanity is exposed to the tragic possibility of losing immortality too, because the materialistic worldview doesn't want to know anything about the divine-spiritual in human beings.[53]

Now as I mentioned yesterday, this image experience, which becomes a tableau of our whole life on earth from birth to the present moment, this whole experience in the etheric is accompanied by a tremendous feeling of happiness. This is the first experience you have, an extremely pleasant higher experience, the whole world of images permeated with an inner feeling of happiness.

Then, as I also indicated yesterday, you have to be able to let all that you have achieved in imagination, in your own life tableau, disappear from consciousness of your own free will. You must be able to empty your consciousness. And only when your consciousness is empty do you then understand how things really are in the spiritual world. For then you know that all you have seen up until now was not yet the spiritual world, was only an imaginative tableau of the spiritual world. Only now when you have arrived at that level where your consciousness is empty, only now does the spiritual world flow through your sensing thinking, just as the physical world flows through the physical senses. Only now do we begin to attain a real experience of the spiritual world, the spiritual outside world. In our life tableau we only had our inside world. Imaginative cognition only gives us the inner world, which reveals itself to higher cognition as a world of images. It gives us images of the cosmos. The cosmos itself and our own true being, as we were before birth, before earthly existence, only appear in inspiration, when the spiritual world flows into us from outside. However, when we arrive at the creation of an empty consciousness, then our soul is filled at first with just being awake and we must achieve a certain inner peace, an inner quietness in this state of just being awake.[54]

Re-experiencing the Inner Child

In the following detailed description—from a lecture given in Stuttgart—Steiner again goes into the relationship between the experience of the tableau and that of the small child, which he already described in the French course. He speaks here of the possibility of extinguishing the tableau 'in the same moment' that we evoke it. Then after describing in detail life before birth, he continues with the descent of the soul into earthly existence, which we have already encountered as Neoplatonic thought.

If you attain imaginative cognition—I won't go into this here, I have often described how you can achieve it—then the first experience is that your physical earthly life is spread out before you like one great tableau. In ordinary physical consciousness your earthly life exists only as a memory in your soul. What therefore is memory? It is something that consists of images, which through their own inner being point to experiences which you have been through in the time since birth or a little later. But they are still images and, through our knowledge of ordinary life as human beings on earth today, we can say that these images cannot exist independently of the physical body. Modern physical science is right in pointing out that these memory images are dependent on the constitution of the physical body. They are right to assert that memory doesn't exist for human beings in the first years of life, that it develops with the physical organism and then fades when the human physical organism approaches its final stage. And from certain symptoms, from studies of the physical organism of sick people after their death, science can also contend that certain aspects of the physical organization are involved in memory deficiency. Of course, science has not yet reached any definite conclusions in this respect, but anyone who has studied the tendency of the relevant findings can already foresee how the time will come, when science will be able to prove how the ordinary images of memory are closely linked to the physical human organism.

But what we have as the flow of experiences, which we see in reverse when we look back on our life, and which surface as separate remembered images, this is not what is meant when I say that in imaginative cognition we have before us our earthly life in its soul-spiritual aspect in a great tableau. What we see in imaginative cognition are truly not such abstract memory images as are stored in ordinary memory. What confronts imaginative cognition is rather an organic experience, intrinsically active, without the passivity of remembered images; something that has an inner power similar to the forces of growth active in our organism when we consume organic matter from the outside world as food and, I'd like to say, miraculously transform it into what we need to make up our organism. What creatively lives and weaves in us is different from what exists more passively in our memory images. Look at thoughts. They illuminate our consciousness and indeed in our earthly existence we owe this life of thought a great debt. In effect it is through it that we become human and only through these thought images do we become fully aware of our human dignity. But they are still fleeting images, tied to the human physical organism as the flame is tied to the fuel of the candle. What someone with imaginative cognition perceives as soul-spiritual life, the basis of physical earthly existence, as a great and wonderful tableau is not passive but has an intrinsic vitality. It is something that confronts us soul-spiritually, but which we recognize through direct soul perception, just as we recognize through our eyes that an object is red. And in imaginative cognition we can say that we don't just have thoughts which flash up in our consciousness, but that we even become aware of such forces at work in our organism.

Many people resented the fact—it is almost absurd—that I once argued, in my little book, *The Spiritual Guidance of Man and of Mankind*, that all the wisdom of adults is nothing compared to the wisdom of a small child. However, this wisdom lives unconsciously in the child. You just have to look with real knowledge, with real understanding at a human brain, a whole human organism in the first years of life and observe how internally human beings then form themselves. The work of even the most brilliant sculptor is insignificant in comparison to what, through the inner soul-spiritual power of the child, forms and sculpts the brain. If you reflect on this, then you will begin to get an idea of the mysterious wisdom at work here, a wisdom which is powerful and not just something stored in a human head to explain the world. This is a wisdom containing within itself an organism of soul-spiritual forces, which continuously permeate the external organism of the child and make it into a whole human being. Just try to imagine in your mind what is working there full of wisdom and brilliance, which humans with their reason and their intellectualistic wisdom can't begin to match. Look at what is at work in the child, what works for years unconsciously, for example, on introducing the miracle of human speech. Try to picture this wise work—it will only be an abstract image—up until that point where the human being becomes sufficiently conscious to be able to use their intelligence. Then, if I can put it this way, this intelligence creates an ephemeral wisdom in imitation of that wisdom, which has created us out of innermost world forces. But we must also be quite clear that even though we develop our human intellectual reason in the upper layer of our being, in the lower levels that force, which formed and shaped our organism so wisely and wonderfully in childhood, continues to hold sway. This basic system, this organism of forces, this is what we perceive as a unitary tableau in imaginative cognition.

Imaginative cognition doesn't perceive abstract remembered pictures, which are bound to the organism, so that you couldn't say whether they would remain if this organism disintegrated into its component parts. This imaginative cognition perceives the system of forces, which builds up the organism and therefore is as little dependent on it as the creative power of the sculptor is dependent on their material. For the material to become what it should become it needs the artistic-creative power of the sculptor. For human beings to become physical organisms, as we are in earthly existence, we need these extra-physical, supersensible forces, the governing soul-spiritual organization which lies behind our human physical existence.

This is the first thing we have to learn to understand when we progress to imaginative cognition.

When we are able to perceive the soul-spiritual working in us during our earthly life, which is not only independent of the physical organism, but actually creates the form of this physical organism, in the moment that we achieve this we also become able to leave this earthly existence, or to use a logical expression, to abstract from it as we would abstract from a thought in physical life. Through those meditation exercises I have often mentioned, we have to acquire the faculty of not only being able to leave a thought, not only being able to suppress a thought, but also of being able to obliterate from our consciousness what we have first put all our effort into attaining: this vision of the soul-spiritual in physical earthly life, this powerful thought tableau.

When we are able to extinguish what we are in our soul, in our spirit during earthly life, to extinguish it also from our inner vision in cognitive selflessness, cognitive altruism, only then does our true soul-spiritual being appear. Only then does what we were before we descended from the soul-spiritual worlds into this physical earthly life appear before our consciousness as a manifest soul-spiritual being. We learn to see ourselves as a soul-spiritual human being in pre-earthly existence. And we learn to speak of this pre-earthly existence not only in general, abstract terms, but to see it in its development—and it is this development which I will describe in part today.

You see, when we speak about ourselves here in earthly life, we feel ourselves connected to our physical body; in our waking state we feel connected to our physical body. As dull as this feeling of connection with the physical body may be, still it exists and it becomes especially apparent when there is some illness in this physical body. Then, we not only have a dull sense of the physical body in general, but can feel individual parts of it. Possibly we can feel our lungs, or our stomach or our heart, the organs of our head. In normal life all that is doused in a dull sense of the life of the body, but unless we're the epitome of good health all our lives, we will have the opportunity to sense individual organs. In short, when we have a sense of ourselves in consciousness during our waking life between birth and death, we feel we belong together with the physical body, with all that is enclosed in our skin. But when we are not connected to our physical earthly life, in those periods when we lead a pure soul-spiritual existence *before* descending into physical earthly life, then it is not our physical body or its various parts that are self-evidently our insides. But we still have an inside. I have already spoken to you of the pictures the soul has between falling asleep and waking up, even though they are not conscious. But in the state the soul was in before descending out of soul-spiritual into physical existence, it was aware of a different inwardness. This awareness of a different inwardness is just hidden, masked by the fact that in our physical earthly life our physical body also becomes an organ of perception. And this obscures the soul's looking into itself, which is only possible when it is free of the body. What the soul experiences as its inwardness is not the same as what is enclosed in the skin of the physical body; rather it is the organization of the cosmos. Just as it's true that we are connected in this physical earthly life with our lungs, our stomach, our heart and with our various other bodily organs, so we are connected in our supersensible existence with what otherwise appears to our eyes and to our other sense organs as the external world of the cosmos. What constitutes the external world when we are in earthly life, becomes for us the inner world when we exist outside earthly life. And from the supersensible existence we lead between death and a new birth, we look down on earthly existence as if it were an outside world. Just as here we are incarnated, so to speak, in our lungs, in our heart and so on, so before we descend into physical earthly life we are embodied in what appears as an external reflection in the movements of the planets, in the constellations of the fixed stars, the forces that flow and weave in the cosmos. What the external world of the cosmos is during our earthly existence becomes our inner world when we are in that life outside of the body.

Don't let the thought put you off, that for all earthly human beings, who all have different bodies, the external world is one and the same. This is exactly the important point, that we all have a common world, when we are in life beyond the earth. The world one person has is the same as the other one has, and human beings—who here in life on earth are separated spatially by the fact that each one is enclosed in their skin are there differentiated by their own soul's power. In life beyond the earth each one of us is still an individuality, but we are, then, not separated from other individualities by space, but by our own inner soul's power, through our inner forces of coherence. And into these forces of coherence flows what corresponds spiritually to the universe, what appears to us as the physical image of the sun, the moon, the planets and the fixed stars.

Here in life on earth we encounter a human being with our external senses, we see the form of their face, the shine of their eyes, the movements of their limbs. However, through the fact that we are ourselves soul-spiritual beings, we are aware that in their facial form, in the shine of their eyes, in the flesh tone of their skin, in the movements of their limbs there lives a soul-spiritual being. Similarly, if we are able to view the world in a soul-spiritual way, we realize that it isn't true, when people say that the sun, the moon, the fixed stars and the planets and the movements of the planets are only what our modern physical astronomy describes. To claim this is similar to describing only the change of position of a facial muscle or the movement of the eyelashes and not wanting to see in that change in position of the facial muscle or the movement of the eyelashes an expression of a soul-spiritual being. If you are able to view the world in a soul-spiritual way you will see in the phenomena of the moon or the sun exactly that physiognomic expression of a cosmic soul-spiritual, just as you see in a human countenance the expression of a soul-spiritual being. In the movements of the planets you see an expression of soul-spiritual events, just as you see in the movements of the limbs of a human being an expression of soul-spiritual impulses. When we were supersensible beings, before we descended into earthly existence, we lived in this soul-spiritual source of what appears as a physical image in the external physical sun, the external physical moon, in the stars and their movements, in this soul-spiritual, which corresponds in the cosmos to the soul-spiritual of the individual human being. And just as I can say as a human being here on earth that the lungs and the heart exist in me, so as a human being beyond the earth, before I descend into physical life in the flesh and form my physical body, I can say that the sun and moon exist in me. I just have to be aware that I don't mean the physical earthly reflection of the sun and the moon, but the soul-spiritual that lies behind them. The whole divine spiritual world lives and weaves in me, when I exist as a human being beyond the earth. When we really understand this, we begin to have a deep veneration for all real-world existence with which we are intertwined. This is because we begin to understand the wonderful relationships which exist between humanity and the universe. We learn to look at human beings, standing there in their physical earthly lives and to say to ourselves: there lives, in what is enclosed in the skin, not only what you can see with your physical eye, or what, after death, a pathologist would see on the dissecting table and would try to understand, but there lives also the goal of all cosmic activity. Those wonderful words of ancient religious times, that the human being is made in the image of God, now gain a new significance and intensity. Inspirative cognition teaches us to turn our gaze towards what we human beings actually experience in our life before birth in relation to the divine-spiritual powers, which lie behind the cosmos.

If we look only at earthly human life, then science speaks first of the human seed which develops out of the body of the mother into the physical human body of the growing child. We refer, as a matter of course, to the seed as something small which gradually grows larger. In our existence before earthly life we also live in a sort of seed, only this includes the whole soul-spiritual cosmos. We become, in a way, one with the whole soul-spiritual cosmos. The divine spiritual powers exist in us, they live and weave in us, they permeate us and form in us the spiritual seed containing those forces, which pass through spiritual existence, and into birth, respectively. Then they appear again as we start to form our own physical organism, as we become our own inner sculptors in earthly life. The miracle of the human form, the human organism becomes clear. This physical organism is the purpose of what we humans experience, when we are fully conscious and capable of a sublime soul-spiritual vision of the cosmic seed in our inner life. We receive the physical seed from the physical world; we receive the spiritual seed from the spiritual world. And in the time before we descend to physical earthly existence, we are, in a certain way, a huge soul-spiritual human seed, spread out over the whole world, that then unites with the physical human seed, which receives us here when we descend to earthly life.

When we look at our life before birth through inspirative cognition, then we see our cosmic existence. Just as here we know we are one with our physical organism, so, through this vision, we know that we are one with the whole world. Here in this world we look at the external revelations of the spiritual in Nature, in human existence; we sense the divine-spiritual behind these physical revelations. In pre-earthly life the divine spiritual existence flows through us, permeates us, saturates us. And this divine-spiritual existence lives in us in such a way that it implants those forces which tend towards physical earthly life. Here on earth we raise our eyes to the wonder of the starry heavens; in our existence beyond the earth we raise our eyes to the wonder of the human physical body, which exists on the earth. I could say, we look from the earth into the heavens in our earthly existence; in our pre-earthly existence we look from the heavens to the earth. Thus, we can begin to understand the earth as the work of the gods, the way it was meant to live in our souls. And all this you experience directly in life before earthly existence.

After we have lived in this pre-earthly existence for a while, then something like a withdrawal of the divine-spiritual beings from us humans takes place. In this soul-spiritual existence we don't yet have nature around us, we don't have physical eyes or any physical organs and so couldn't perceive nature even if it were there. We only have around us a kind of divine-spiritual illumination. This is the great turnaround in pre-earthly existence. At first we are steeped in divine-spiritual life, we directly experience divine spiritual beings, but then there comes a point where we look with our spiritual eyes into the spiritual world around us, which is still the spiritual world, but we must say to ourselves: formerly we lived with divine-spiritual beings, but now they reveal themselves to us through their deeds, now their actions are there. These are soul-spiritual actions, that we don't perceive after entering earthly life, but still they are just a manifestation of what we formerly experienced ourselves. We leave the sphere of experience and enter the sphere of manifestation. And to the same degree that we relinquish experience for manifestation, we have to say to ourselves: the soul-spiritual beings have withdrawn from us humans, from our direct experience, now we can only have a vision of them. They are certainly there but only for our soul-spiritual vision. In this same moment there awakens in our soul-spiritual, pre-birth existence something which I can only compare to what lives in our physical organism as desire. As human beings we are permeated inwardly by desire to the same degree that the world becomes pre-earthly manifestation. Only now do we start to experience ourselves as a self that is separated from the rest of the world. We are leaving that experience of ourselves as human beings that is simultaneously an experience of the world. For a time between death and a new birth we are not only human beings, we are world beings. World consciousness and human consciousness are united. Then the time comes when world consciousness and human consciousness diverge and we no longer experience the world, it only manifests itself to us, and an inwardness appears in us, which is separate from the world. Before our inner self was one with the world; now there appears an inner self separate from the world and this is heralded by an inner desire, a willing and wanting. Willing, wanting, desiring always has a goal. This willing, wanting, desiring has as its goal our future earthly life, to which we will eventually descend. We are filled with visions of our future earthly life and in this way, we receive those forces, which become unconscious when we pass through the life of the embryo on earth. At first we are conscious of them, but consciousness becomes gradually weaker and then at a certain point desire becomes strong and even the manifestations of the soul-spiritual world, where we had lived and weaved before, become darker and darker. Then as soul-spiritual beings in pre-earthly existence we have to say to ourselves: the spiritual world around us is becoming increasingly shadowy. What formerly shone brilliantly as divine revelation is becoming a shadow. To the same extent that the outside world becomes more and more a shadow, so the inner forces of desire become increasingly vehement. The outside world becomes darker for us in our spiritual existence, the inner world becomes stronger and after a time this strong inner world obscures our awareness of our future earthly life. For a time, shortly before earthly conception, our vision of earthly existence becomes obscured. Previously we could look at our earthly existence; in a way it was the purpose of that mighty world tableau in which we have lived. Now our vision of the earth is slipping away, we have instead a different one. Not long before we descend to earth, just as we descend, our vision of the earth slips away and instead we have a vision of the etheric world. We can perceive the ether phenomena, which manifest as light, as the life forces, and this etheric world which is spread out in space, not centrally from the earth up to space, but working, flowing as if from the periphery of the world on to the earth, becomes visible to us. As if in a great world mist, which contains in itself the most diverse formations, the etheric world surrounding us becomes spiritually visible. And with that power remaining to us, with the force of desire, we can take from this universal etheric world our own etheric body; we can form it and by forming our own etheric body, we shape with it an image of what we once were in the soul-spiritual world. We integrate this etheric body into the physical substance offered us through inheritance, through lineage, through our ancestors and then we descend into earthly existence.[55]

The Cosmic Dimension: Wisdom of the Individual Life Epochs

As mentioned in the last lecture excerpt, inspirative cognition, which develops out of the life tableau, is linked to the spheres of the planets. In a lecture held in 1924, Steiner describes at length how we can carry out the inspirative erasure of the life tableau step by step, always concentrating on the respective life epoch and how, through this, we then come into contact with the corresponding planet sphere.

However, we must take into account the specific context in which Steiner is speaking about the life tableau here. He slips these remarks into one of his lectures on the karma of historic personalities, in order to show how he arrived at certain insights about their karma. This also demonstrates how, in the higher stages of supersensible cognition, the life panorama can be used as a tool for further research.

Now, so that these ideas can mutually support each other, I'd like to explain how someone studying modern initiation science arrives at such findings. I have often described, recently even in public lectures, how having achieved actual supersensible cognition using the methods you will find in my book, *How to Know Higher Worlds*, you, at first, look back on your earthly life and see this as in a tableau. Everything that is usually inside you in consecutive order is now in front of you simultaneously as a mighty life panorama, that you can see up until the birth of the I; but the various life epochs or periods are in a certain sense separated. You look at what you experienced from birth until the second teeth; you look back and see, as a closed series, what happened from the second teeth until puberty, then again up until your twenties and so on. But as you make progress in your concentration by continuing to apply the methods for knowing the spiritual world to your own development, then you will arrive at a point when by looking at the life tableau you see not only what one can see there, but first what goes from birth to the seventh year and later how this life tableau in a way disappears; in a certain sense you are seeing *through* your own life. Now if you have attained empty consciousness, inspirative cognition, there appears in lieu of your own life, meaning here early childhood, where you had previously seen what you experienced from birth until you were seven, the living, weaving sphere of the moon. Thus, for a normal modern initiation, when you extinguish your own life tableau with inspirative cognition and then see what shines through in place of your own experiences of life between birth and your seventh year, initiation science allows you to perceive the mysteries of the moon sphere.

Then if you look back at what you lived through from your seventh until your fourteenth year and then extinguish it in inspirative cognition, then you see into the Mercury sphere. Everything is linked to the human being. We are connected to the whole of the universe. If we learn to really know ourselves, if we can find our way in ourselves, then we get to know the whole universe.

And now I ask you to consider the following. We can really have great respect for the old, instinctive science of initiation. This science gave things the right names, names which we still use today. If we gave only some of these things names today, we would see what chaos would ensue, because with our modern cognition and knowledge we can't compose suitable names. But if we observe life without prejudice, we will have respect, veneration for what the old science of initiation achieved. This science knew from instinct what today we can determine through all kinds of statistics: that when we are very young, we human beings have childhood illnesses, we are very susceptible to illness and die easily. Then we are again as susceptible only after puberty. The healthiest period of life is during the years from seven to fourteen; mortality is very low then. This is the effect of the Mercury sphere. The old wisdom knew this and today we begin to recognize it again, when we penetrate the mysteries of existence through modern initiation science. We should bow deeply before what we can discover in the ancient sacred traditions of humanity.

Then when you look back at what you experienced between your fourteenth and your twentieth year and you extinguish it in inspirative cognition, then you will enter into the mysteries of the Venus sphere. Again, you see the wonderful workings of the old science of initiation. The human being becomes sexually mature, love appears. When we look with the knowledge of old initiation science then we can see how we enter the period where the secrets of Venus are revealed. All these things that can be described in the way I have done here, are part of real human self-knowledge, deepened human self-knowledge, which develops in this manner.

Then again when you look back to the time between your twenty-first and forty-second years and then extinguish your own imaginative experience through inspirative cognition, then you come to the mysteries of the sun sphere. As I have indicated in my previous arguments, now in the review of the time between your twenty-first and your forty-second years, through deepening self-knowledge you can attain real knowledge of the sun. To attain knowledge of the sun you have to look through a life span three times as long as for the other heavenly bodies of our planetary system. And you have to take that literally. If I said to you that a personality of world history has worked through their karma primarily in the spheres of Mercury and Venus, now you can see how to investigate something like this. You use the possibility of looking back on your own life in the period between the seventh and the fourteenth year and then between the fourteenth and the twenty-first; then you extinguish these in inspiration and thus attain insight into the spheres of Mercury and of Venus. Through these insights you can see how such an individuality works together with other beings of the higher hierarchies and with other human souls and how through this they bring about their earthly incarnation, an earthly incarnation in the nineteenth century. If however, beings have had to work on their karma primarily in the Mars sphere, then it is more difficult to investigate. This is because when someone is initiated before their forty-ninth year, they can't look back to the period in question here, the period from the forty-second to the forty-ninth year. You have to have passed your forty-ninth year in order to extinguish what you were then; then you can look into the secrets of the Mars sphere. And if you were initiated after your fifty-sixth year, then you can look back at another period, namely the period between the forty-ninth and the fifty-sixth years, that period where the karmas of Jupiter are worked through. Now you can see these whole interrelations. Only when you can review the period between the fifty-sixth and the sixty-third year can you see and speak about this whole context from a position of inner knowledge, as there you can look back at the profoundly remarkable Saturn sphere.[56]

Each life epoch is connected to a certain planetary sphere and extinguishing a certain life period in one's own life tableau leads one to the planetary sphere connected to it.

Through the Forces of Childhood to the 'Higher Self' and the Christ Experience

In conclusion we could ask ourselves why in his earlier depictions of the anthroposophic path of meditation—for instance in How to Know Higher Worlds *or* An Outline of Esoteric Science—*Rudolf Steiner didn't give us the description of the life tableau, which we have documented here in detail, and which he started to speak of only in 1920.*

For a start it is striking that what is described in How to Know Higher Worlds *and in many other depictions*[57] *is a path towards the outside, a path leading to a deeper perception and understanding of nature. In many basic texts however, above all in* An Outline of Esoteric Science, *there are instructions for meditation not associated with nature. These are word or image meditations. This form of meditation is concerned not with nature, but has to do with directly intensifying thinking and hence the etheric experience of the consciousness aspect of the etheric body.*

Around 1920 Steiner added the description of the life tableau to this path towards the inside. We can experience the life tableau because we can experience the other side, the life side of the etheric body, which has to do with memory and which on a soul level is connected to our will—provided we have practised the necessary will exercises, beginning with the retrospective one, as extensively as the meditation exercises.

The life tableau experience is a kind of imaginative memory, which we aren't aware of in normal consciousness. Imaginative experience leads us to those life processes, which form the foundations of our memory and which run parallel to each process of perception, albeit unconsciously. The life tableau shows, so to speak, the entirety of these life processes which are concentrated in memory.[58]

In order to realize the life tableau in meditation we need to have achieved two things: firstly, an intensification of thinking through which the transformation of life forces into ordinary thinking and conceiving is brought to a halt, so that thinking itself can function like a life force. Secondly, a kind of reversion of the will in the retrospective exercise, through which we can experience as if from outside the movements lying behind our own will. In this way we prepare and aid the forming of memory, which is really a process of forgetting, taking place mainly in sleep. If we extend our daily retrospect to include our whole life or at least particular periods of our life, then this exercise coupled with intensified thinking can lead to the experience of the life tableau. In this tableau there appears the sum of our life forces as they have developed over the course of our life. And thus, we relive what we experienced as small children, namely the life forces which have formed our corporeal existence, but have not yet been transformed into thinking and conceiving.

In his short book published in 1911, The Spiritual Guidance of Mankind, *Steiner links this experience to the Christ forces. In the first chapter he describes in detail the forming of the human body, especially of the brain, in early childhood and continues:*

A thought emerges from this which has great significance if we understand it aright. It is expressed in the New Testament in the following words: 'Except ye become as little children, ye shall not enter the kingdom of heaven!' If we accept this as true, then what is the highest ideal for human beings? It must be this: that we gradually achieve a conscious relationship to those forces which work unconsciously in human beings in the first years of childhood. But we have to take into account that we would collapse under the weight of these forces if they worked upon our conscious lives without any preparation. This is why it is necessary to prepare ourselves conscientiously for acquiring those powers which allow us to perceive the supersensible worlds. The aim of this preparation is to make us able to endure what we can't endure in normal life.[59]

And Steiner continues:

The object of development through successive earthly lives is therefore to make the whole human being, including the conscious part, into an expression of those forces which we aren't conscious of, but which with the help of the spiritual world rule over us in our first years of life. In the light of this we must in all humility and regard for human dignity allow the following thought to fill our souls: human beings are not alone. Something lives in us which can prove to us again and again that we can rise above ourselves, we can become what already rises beyond us and what will continue to grow from one life to another. This thought forms itself more and more clearly, it comforts and elevates us, but it also fills the soul with the appropriate modesty and humility. What does this mean, what do we have in us? We can truly feel that a higher, a divine human being permeates us and we say to ourselves: this is my guide within me.

Considering this we easily arrive at the thought that we should do all that we can to be in harmony with that human being in us, that is wiser than our conscious intelligence. And our conscious self refers to a higher self in whose light all our false pride, all our self-conceit can be reduced and redeemed. This feeling develops into a proper understanding of our present imperfection and it lets us see how we can become more perfect, when one day that more comprehensive spirituality which reigns in us will be able to have the same relationship to our consciousness as it does in the first years of childhood to the unconscious life of the soul.[60]

We can actually achieve this relationship to the forces at work in early childhood through the imaginative life tableau. For we become conscious of these forces and their effect on the stage of imagination through intensifying and transforming the powers of thinking.

Steiner continues: in human life these formative forces can only work on us in the first three years, we couldn't cope with them longer than that as they are extremely powerful. Nevertheless, these powers lived in a completely conscious adult human being for exactly three years: in the body of Jesus of Nazareth.

As the I of Jesus of Nazareth left the three bodies, the human organism, which received baptism in the Jordan from John, held in complete consciousness that higher human self, which otherwise works with cosmic wisdom on the child, who is not conscious of it. But this made it inevitable that this self, which was connected to the higher spiritual world, could only live in the relevant human organism for three years. The reality was that after three years the earthly life of this being was over.

You have to understand the external events of the life of Christ Jesus in such a way that they are brought about by these inner causes I have described. They are the *external expression* of these causes.

This is the deeper relationship between what is the guide in us humans, what works in the dark in our childhood, what is always at work under the surface of our consciousness as the best in us and between what appeared only once in the whole of human evolution, so that it could spend three years in a human form. [. . .] To recognize the forces at work in the early years of the child means to recognize the Christ in human beings.[61]

In two lectures held in 1911 after the publication of The Spiritual Guidance of Mankind *Steiner links these childhood forces to our own angel. The 'guide in me' becomes here the guardian angel. And the relationship, which we can establish with these childhood forces through our experience of the life tableau, is, at the same time, the relationship we can have with our angel.*

It is an extremely important fact that the first three years of life are very different from later years and we have to view the human being as a completely different being in those first years than they are later. The human I to which everything is connected doesn't appear until later. But nobody should claim that this I was inactive before. Of course, it wasn't inactive. It doesn't first get born in the third year of life; it was always there, but it had another task and not that of influencing consciousness.

What was this task? This is the most important spiritual factor in the formation of the child's three sheaths, the astral body, the etheric body and the physical body. The physical sheath of the brain is continually being reshaped. There we have the I constantly at work. It can't become conscious because it has a completely different task: it has to form this tool of consciousness. The same thing, which later becomes conscious, works first on our physical brain in the first three years. This is only a change in the task of the I. First it works *on* us, then *in* us. At first this I is really a sculptor and it is incredible what it achieves in forming this physical brain. This I is a magnificent artist. But who gives it this power? It has this power because in the first three years of life the powers of the next higher hierarchy, the angels, flow into this I. In reality—and this is not an image or an analogy but in fact a truth—through the human I our angel is at work in us, a being of the next higher hierarchy. This being works in the I and through the I on the human being and moulds and forms us. It is as if we had the whole current of spiritual life, as if we flowed up to the higher hierarchies and there the powers of the higher hierarchies streamed into us. And in that moment where we learn to say I, then it is as if some of this power is cut off, as if we ourselves are called to do some of what previously the angel did.[62]

Then we receive the answer, that the I is guided in its tasks by beings of the higher hierarchies. If we look at a child using our visionary powers then their I exists as an I-aura, but from this I-aura rays flow out to the higher hierarchies, to the angels, archangels and so on, and in turn the powers of the hierarchies flow into it. Thus, if someone says in a naïve way that the child is protected by an angel then this is a very real truth. Later on, this close association comes to an end, the I experiences itself more in the nerves and can become aware of itself. This is a kind of cutting off. We have in the human child a kind of 'telephone connection', whereby the I continues on into the divine-spiritual hierarchies.[63]

Here Steiner alludes to a relationship which he doesn't explicitly mention in his descriptions of the life tableau, but based on the excerpts above we must assume it is always implicitly there. For the life tableau leads, when it is extinguished in the subsequent step, to the 'higher self' referred to here, which is really the soul as it existed in the spiritual world before birth. In the end it is this true self that expresses itself in the life tableau and which is, at the same time, the work of our angel or guardian angel. The consciousness of the angel is actually always tableau-like, otherwise they couldn't be our 'guide', who is wiser than we in our everyday consciousness are. And it is the angel who makes the connection to the world of the higher hierarchies and ultimately to the Christ forces.

Here Steiner shows an inward, mystical path, which is known in the Christian tradition as the 'mystical marriage' of the soul with the Christ. This is a union that Christian meditation since the times of the desert fathers and mothers has aspired to, in mystical prayer and in mystical contemplation.[64] *However, Steiner clearly distances anthroposophic meditation, in as far as it leads to the life tableau, from this older form of mysticism, which having a stronger connection to the body merely results in a mirroring of inner body processes. But at the same time, he makes it clear that the imaginative experience of the tableau brought about by enhanced cognition is a modern anthroposophic form of the mystical experience.*

With strengthened soul forces the mystic enters more deeply into their own being than they would with just normal memory. Through the strengthened forces of the soul they can, in a way, break through the wall of mirrors. There they encounter areas of their own organization, which you can't reach with the usual processes of memory. The forces of these areas participate in the forming of memory, but they remain unconscious. Only their *effect* appears in the fact that the memory image is slightly different from the immediate experience. But what the mystic gets into their consciousness as the *cause* of this effect, they experience as if it were a memory. It has the image nature of a memory. However, while the latter reproduce experiences which once happened in our earthly life, but at the moment of remembering no longer exist, the mystic experience images which were never earthly events. In the form of thought memory, they experience a world of images which is *not* memory.

When we approach these things through anthroposophic research, then we realize that the processes of one's own body are revealed in the mystic images gained in the aforementioned way. This takes place in a kind of symbolism similar to that of dream images. We can say that the mystic dreams of the processes of their own physical organization.

This revelation will, of course, be a bitter disappointment for those who see mysticism differently. But someone who wants to enter into the mysteries of the real world will welcome every form of knowledge and therefore also the fact that, in a certain soul sense, physical processes appear as of the same fabric as our nightly dreams. And following on from this we can see that this is a guarantee for the fact that the human physical organization has its origins in the wellspring of the soul.[65]

As anthroposophic researchers we have to be aware of these things; we have to understand the methods and perspectives of mysticism. But our path is a different one. We don't break through directly into the memory mirror and thus into the physical organization. We transform the forces of memory while they are still soul-spiritual, still thought forces. We do this by concentrating these forces and by the way we meditate with them. With strongly concentrated soul forces we focus our attention on clear ideas. In this way we strengthen these forces *within* the region of the soul, while the mystic immerses him or herself in the region of the physical body.

Thus, anthroposophic researchers arrive at the contemplation of an etheric body, the body of formative forces, which is connected as a higher body to the physical one. Mystics end up *dreaming* about the physical body; anthroposophic researchers arrive at a super-physical reality. This body of formative forces no longer exists in spatial forms—it lives in a purely temporal form. In contrast to the spatial physical body it's a *temporal body*. Initially it shows those forces, which have been at work in the physical body during your earthly life, as a tableau in their chronological development, but perceptible all at the same time. It is clearly different from a mere comprehensive memory image in a particular moment of our earthly lives up to that point. Such a memory image shows, rather, the way in which the world and other people approached the person remembering; the life tableau, however, contains the sum of the impulses rising out of the person themselves and all the accompanying entanglement, sympathy and antipathy, with which this person approached the world and other people. Hence it shows how the person moulded their own life. The relationship of the life tableau to the memory image is like that of the engraving in the signet ring to the impression it makes in the wax.

In this life tableau you have the first object of anthroposophical research; starting from here you can then take it further.[66]

Now it is clear that the intensification of the power of thinking and its transformation has evidently only become possible for modern scientific consciousness. So the path to this consciousness was, at the same time, a path that freed thinking from nature to such an extent that it can now grasp itself. Steiner captured this connection with the concept of the 'consciousness soul', which followed the rational soul. Returning to our original question, namely the two paths described by Steiner, one outwards and the other inwards, it becomes apparent that on the one hand he specified meditations of perception, in which transformed thinking in relation to external nature leads to a merging with the natural formative forces and thus to a deeper experience of nature. This path continues today in the ongoing research into formative force.[67] *The other path however, which you can follow through the word meditations and the accompanying will exercises Steiner has given in great number,*[68] *leads inwards to the imaginative life tableau described here. Both paths belong essentially together as both lead into the world of the etheric: to the formative forces of nature and to the formative forces of our own life.*

At the end of his life Steiner juxtaposed both these paths deliberately in the letters 'To the Members', by referring on the side of nature or outwards to the Michael being and on the other side or inwards to the Christ. With this perspective we will bring to a close this selection of texts on developing the life tableau through the practice of meditation.

Michael will give us the proper orientation when we are dealing with the world surrounding us, whether in action or in pursuit of knowledge. But we have to find the path to Christ inside ourselves.

We can readily understand that in a time where knowledge of nature has taken the form it has in the last five centuries, knowledge of the supersensible world has become as we now experience it today.

Nature has to be perceived and experienced in such a

way that it is empty of gods. But human beings can no longer experience themselves in such a relationship to the world. In as far as we are supersensible beings, the position assigned us by modern science in relation to nature reveals *nothing* about ourselves. And if we only focus on this position, then we cannot live the ethical life appropriate to our humanity.

This gives us reason enough not to allow this way of life and these methods of cognition to flow into anything connected to the supersensible human being or indeed the supersensible world as a whole. We must isolate this world altogether from what is accessible through ordinary human cognition. We draw on a world of knowledge revealed in ways above and beyond scientific methods.

But we also have the purely spiritual activity of the Christ. Since the mystery of Golgotha Christ is accessible for the human soul. And the soul's relationship to Christ doesn't have to be just a dimly mystic-type feeling; it can become a completely real connection which we can experience deeply and clearly.

From this community with Christ, however, there then flows into the human soul what we need to know about our own supersensible being. We must perceive this as our living experience of the Christ flowing constantly into the revelations of faith. Our lives become Christianized by experiencing the Christ as that being who gives our human soul the realization of its own supersensible nature.

Thus, we can place the Michael-experience and the Christ-experience next to each other. Through Michael we will find the proper way into the supersensible with regard to external nature. Without being distorted in any way, knowledge of nature will take its rightful place next to a spiritual view of the world and of human beings, in as far as we are world beings.

When we have the right relationship to Christ, what we would otherwise only receive through traditional faith revelations is revealed in our living soul relationship with Christ. We can experience the inner world of soul life as spirit-illuminated and the outer world of nature as spirit-borne.[69]

Notes

For consistency of language and style, German texts from Rudolf Steiner have been translated afresh. Thus, page references refer to the German editions. However, published English translations, listed by the Collected Works ('GA' number), are given on p. 146.

1. You can find out more about the life tableau in: Rudolf Steiner: *Life beyond Death*, compiled and edited by Frank Teichmann, Rudolf Steiner Press, 1995; also in further lectures, above all in *The Inner Nature of Man and Our Life between Death and Rebirth*, GA 153, 2013.
2. You can find first indications of this, for example, in the lecture on 2 January 1916 (in GA 165) or in the essay 'Frühere Geheimhaltung und jetzige Veröffentlichung übersinnliche Erkenntnisse' from 1918 (in GA 35).
3. Cf. from the series 'Die kleinen Begleiter': *Rudolf Steiner: Erkenne dich selbst*, edited by Andreas Neider, Dornach 2010.
4. Rudolf Steiner: Lecture given in Dornach, 8 September 1922, GA 215, p. 48.
5. Rudolf Steiner/Ita Wegman: *Extending Practical Medicine*, GA 27, London 2000, p. 12.
6. Cf. Rudolf Steiner: *How to Know Higher Worlds*, GA 10, or the series 'Die kleinen Begleiter' in which numerous volumes on Rudolf Steiner's meditation exercises have appeared.
7. Cf. For example Thich Nhat Hanh: *Reconciliation: Healing the Inner Child*, 2006.
8. Erika Chopich and Margaret Paul: *Healing Your Aloneness: Finding Love and Wholeness through Your Inner Child*, 1990. See also trauma-therapy approaches such as those summarized in

Jochen Peichl: *Innere Kinder, Täter, Helfer & Co. Ego-State-Therapie des traumatisierten Selbst*, Stuttgart 2007. See also on the popularity of this approach the Spiegel bestseller by Stefanie Stahl: *Das Kind in dir muss Heimat finden*, Munich, 2015.

9. Cf. the volume from the series 'Themenwelten': Rudolf Steiner: *Gedächtnis, Erinnerung und Vergessen*, edited by Andreas Neider, Basel 2016.
10. Lecture given in Dornach, 2 October 1920, GA 322, p.80.
11. Anthroposophic psychotherapy does work with memories, which have been lost or repressed, but doesn't however include the imaginative life tableau. See the excellent and comprehensive volume from Ad Dekkers: *A Psychology of Human Dignity*, 2016. On the status quo of anthroposophic psychotherapy see also Johannes Reiner (Editor): *In der Nacht sind wir zwei Menschen. Arbeitseinblicke in die anthroposophische Psychotherapie*, Stuttgart 2012, and also Wolf-Ulrich Klünker, Johannes Reiner u.a.: *Psychologie des Ich. Anthroposophie, Psychotherapie*, Stuttgart 2016, as well as the volume edited by Harald Haas: *Self-Doubt: Depression, Anxiety Disorders, Panic and Fear*, 2018.

    Since the 1980s, based on further remarks by Steiner on the significance of various ages for the development of soul and spirit, the method of anthroposophic biography work has developed. See George and Gisela O'Neil: *Der Lebenslauf: Lesen in der eigenen Biografie*, Stuttgart, 4th edition 2014 (*The Human Life*, Mercury Press, 1990), as well as Gudrun Burkhard: *Das Leben in die Hand nehmen. Arbeit an der eigenen Biografie*, Stuttgart, 16th edition 2014 (*Taking Charge, Your Life Patterns and Their Meaning*, Floris Books, 1997).
12. A. H. Almaas: *Facets of Unity. The Enneagram of Holy Ideas*, Berkeley 1998. Cf. also Sandra Maitri: *The Spiritual Dimension of the Enneagram. Nine Faces of the Soul*, New York 2000.

13. Cf. Werner Beierwaltes: *Das wahre Selbst. Studien zu Plotinus's Begriff des Geistes und des Einen*, Frankfurt a.M. 2001, and Werner Beierwaltes: *Selbsterkenntnis und Erfahrung der Einheit. Plotinus's Enneade V.3*, Frankfurt a.M. 1991. Plato speaks in *Phaedo* about the lost ideas of life before birth and of remembering them again in earthly life, but he sees philosophy, as does Socrates, as an initiation into death. Only with Plotinus does life before birth become the focus of philosophy, as Steiner understands it in the French course.
14. Rudolf Steiner probably met Henri Bergson in April 1911 at the Congress of Philosophy in Bologna, where he held his well-known 'Bologna Lecture' and Bergson spoke on 'Philosophical Intuition'.
15. To clarify Steiner's understanding of time see Andreas Neider: *Der Mensch und das Geheimnis der Zeit. Zum Verständnis der Zeit im Werk Rudolf Steiners*, Stuttgart 2016.
16. *Cosmology, Religion, Philosophy*, GA 25, p. 26.
17. Ibid., p. 24.
18. See Rudolf Steiner: *Gedächtnis, Erinnerung und Vergessen*, edited by Andreas Neider, Basel 2016.
19. Cf. *Mindfulness and Reverence. Steps in Perception*, edited by Andreas Neider, 2017.
20. In his first anthroposophic essay *Mysticism at the Dawn of the Modern Age* Steiner describes the mysticism of Meister Eckhart or Jakob Boehme as a medieval, outdated form of soul vision, which can be renewed and made productive by the natural science revolution of modern times. He is concerned with transforming mystical introspection into a 'mystical' form of the knowledge of nature: 'Some people who lean towards mysticism want to base it not on contemporary scientific knowledge, but on what the texts of this period have to say. Through this however they become strangers to one of the main preoccupations of their time. It might seem as if modern natural science in its true form doesn't show the way to pre-

dispose the soul to find the light of the spirit in mystical contemplation. [. . . . .] In this essay I intend to show that this must not be the case. [. . .] These personalities (such as Nicholas of Cusa) prove that modern natural science is capable of mystical deepening.' (GA 7, Dornach 1987, p. 8.)

21. Cf. *Rückschau. Übungen zur Willensstärkung*, edited by Martina Maria Sam, Dornach 2009. (*Strengthening the Will*, Rudolf Steiner Press, 2010.)
22. Cf. Rudolf Steiner: *Interesse am anderen Menschen*, edited by Andreas Neider, Stuttgart 2006.
23. In these approaches the whole point is to go through *your own* experiences once more, which, in the case of difficult emotional experiences, runs the risk of re-traumatization.
24. Here too there is a difference from those psychotherapeutic methods, which endeavour to transform the negative influences of other people, such as the parents, and, through bringing in fictional persons to turn them into positive, fictional impacts. Cf. The publication already mentioned above from Stefanie Stahl: *Das Kind in dir muss Heimat finden*, Munich, 2015.
25. Lecture given in Berne, 12 December 1918, in GA 186, Dornach 1990 p. 172.
26. Ibid., p. 174.
27. Many of these meditation exercises have appeared in the series published by the Rudolf Steiner Verlag '*Die kleinen Begleiter*'. See i.a. the volumes *Rückschau. Übungen zur Willensstärkung*; *Erkenne dich Selbst*; *Andacht und Achtsamkeit. Stufen des Wahrnehmens*; *Ich bin. Meditationen für den Alltag*; *Meditationen für Tag und Jahr; Die Nebenübungen. Sechs Schritte zur Selbsterziehung.*
28. Lecture given in Dornach, 8 September 1922, GA 215.
29. Lecture given in Dornach, 9 September 1922, GA 215.
30. Lecture given in Dornach, 13 September 1922, GA 215.
31. *Cosmology, Religion and Philosophy*, GA 25.

32. *Cosmology, Religion and Philosophy*, GA 25.
33. *Cosmology, Religion and Philosophy*, GA 25.
34. In a notebook on the lecture from 29 November 1921 in Christiania (Oslo), which will be quoted later on, Steiner writes in this connection: 'Life before birth = the etheric body attracted by the I and the astral body = these have received their indwelling characteristic previously = *the astral body* is filled with thoughts with which it fills the etheric body as the formative body—the *I* is filled with the concentrated power—which is impressed both on the etheric body—as well as later on the phys. body.' (Contribution to the Collected Works of Rudolf Steiner, Volume 21, 1968, p. 14.)
35. *Cosmology, Religion and Philosophy*, GA 25.
36. These exercises are described in several chapters in the written summary of the French Course (GA 25). They basically consist of consciously adopting habits, which we hadn't had before over the course of our lives.
37. *Cosmology, Religion and Philosophy*, GA 25.
38. Lecture given in Dornach, 13 September 1922, GA 215.
39. *Cosmology, Religion and Philosophy*, GA 25.
40. Lecture given in Basel, 2 December 1920, GA 255b.
41. Lecture given in The Hague, 10 April 1922, GA 82.
42. Lecture given in The Hague, 10 April 1922, GA 82.
43. Lecture given in Christiania (Oslo), 25 November 1921, GA 79.
44. Lecture given in Dornach, 9 February 1924, GA 234.
45. Lecture given in Christiania (Oslo), 25 November 1921, GA 79.
46. Lecture given in Christiania (Oslo), 25 November 1921, GA 79.
47. Lecture given in Christiania (Oslo), 26 November 1921, GA 79.
48. Lecture given in Christiania (Oslo), 29 November 1921, GA 79.

49. Lecture given in Christiania (Oslo), 29 November 1921, GA 79.
50. Notebook entry from the year 1921, published in: *Beiträge zur Rudolf Steiner Gesamtausgabe Heft 21*, 1968.
51. Lecture given in Vienna, 27 September 1923, GA 84.
52. Lecture given in Stuttgart, 19 March 1921, GA 324.
53. Lecture given in Penmaenmawr, 19 August 1923, GA 227.
54. Lecture Penmaenmawr, 20 August 1923, GA 227.
55. Lecture given in Stuttgart, 14 October 1922, GA 218.
56 Lecture given in Breslau, 8 June 1924, GA 239.
57. See also *Mindfulness and Reverence, Steps in Perception*, ed. Andreas Neider, 2017.
58. Cf.: *Gedächtnis, Erinnern und Vergessen*, edited by Andreas Neider, Basel, 2016.
59. *Spiritual Guidance of the Individual and Humanity*, GA 15.
60. *Spiritual Guidance of the Individual and Humanity*, GA 15.
61. *Spiritual Guidance of the Individual and Humanity*, GA 15.
62. Lecture given in Munich, 11 February 1911, GA 127.
63. Lecture given in Zurich, 25 February 1911, GA 127.
64. Cf. the comprehensive depiction of Christian mysticism by Kurt Ruh in: *Geschichte der abendländische Mystik*, four volumes, Munich, 1990–1999, also the general survey of the history of occidental meditation in two volumes by Karl Baier: *Meditation and Modernity*, Würzburg 2009, as well as the essay of the editor: 'Die vier Stufen der christlich-mystischen Meditation. Die "Stufenleiter der Mönche" des Guiges II, als Muster eines westlichen Meditationsweges', in *Die Drei*, October 2016, pp. 1–13.
65. Steiner spoke repeatedly about this form of mysticism, usually he mentions the mystics Teresa of Avila, Mechthild of Magdeburg, Meister Eckhart, John of the Cross and Johannes Tauler, for example in the lecture in Dornach on 3 October 1920, in: *Boundaries of Natural Science*, GA 322, Dornach 1981, pp. 109–127.

66. 'Anthroposophy and Mysticism', in: *Der Goetheeanumgedanke inmitten der Kulturkrisis der Gegenwart: Gesammelte Aufsätze aus der Wochenschrift 'Das Goetheanum' 1921–1925*, GA 36.
67. Cf. Dorian Schmidt: *Life Forces—Formative Forces. Researching the Formative Energy of Life and Growth*, Stroud 2014, and Juergen Strube: *Die Beobachtung des Denkens. Rudolf Steiners 'Philosophie der Freiheit als Weg zur Bildekräfte-Erkenntnis*, Dornach 2010.
68. Cf. *Soul Exercises* (GA 267) with word and symbol meditations as well as mantric sayings. Image meditations such as the Rosicrucian meditation are probably situated between the two types of meditation mentioned here.
69. Letter to the Members, 2 November 1924, in *Anthroposophical Leading Thoughts*, GA 26.

Sources

The following volumes are cited in this book. Where relevant, published editions of equivalent English translations are provided.

The works of Rudolf Steiner are listed with the volume numbers of the complete works in German, the *Gesamtausgabe* (GA), as published by Rudolf Steiner Verlag, Dornach, Switzerland.

RSP = Rudolf Steiner Press, UK
AP / SB = Anthroposophic Press / SteinerBooks, USA

15 *The Spiritual Guidance of the Individual and Humanity* (SB)
25 *Cosmology, Religion and Philosophy* (AP)
26 *Anthroposophic Leading Thoughts* (RSP)
36 *Der Goetheeanumgedanke inmitten der Kulturkrisis der Gegenwart: Gesammelte Aufsätze aus der Wochenschrift 'Das Goetheanum' 1921–1925*
79 *Die Wirklichkeit der höhren Welten*
82 *Damit der Mensch ganz Mensch werde*
84 *Was wollte das Goetheanum und was soll die Anthroposophie?* (English translation, *The Aims of Anthroposophy*, due 2020, RSP)
127 *Die Mission der neuen Geistesoffenbarung. Das Christus-Ereignis als Mittelpunktsgeschehen der Erdenevolution*
215 *Philosophy, Cosmology, and Religion* (AP)
218 *Spirit as Sculptor of the Human Organism* (RSP)
227 *The Evolution of Consciousness* (RSP)
234 *Anthroposophy and the Inner Life* (RSP)
239 *Karmic Relationships*, Vol. V (RSP)
255b *Die Anthroposophie und ihre Gegner 1919–1921*
324 *Anthroposophy and Science* (Mercury Press)

All English-language titles are available via Rudolf Steiner Press, UK (www.rudolfsteinerpress.com) or SteinerBooks, USA (www.steinerbooks.org)